SHOO… …UAL 1974

WHEN Spurs meet Liverpool, the action is always lively. Here, six of the clubs' many international stars tussle for a loose ball. From left: Larry Lloyd (Liverpool), Alan Gilzean (Spurs), Peter Cormack, Chris Lawler, Emlyn Hughes and Martin Peters.

80P

'MY MAGNIFICENT

"WHAT'S it like playing for England?" A question that's often put to me by fans, and one that's difficult to answer briefly. To be selected for one's country is, of course, just about the biggest thing that can happen to a footballer. It's a landmark in your career—the sign that you're recognised as being outstanding in your particular position. You're an international—you play with, and against, the finest players in the game.

A whole new world opens up to the man who dons his country's shirt. A world full of excitement, fame, joy, despair, triumph, tragedy—in short, a world of tremendous contrast.

It's this "contrast" aspect that really struck me as I sat down to write this article.

Overawed

For instance, the difference between being first selected, and being chosen now, after an eleven-year stretch, most of those years as captain.

I can vividly recall the first time I reported for "duty" with the England squad. It was in 1962, I was 21, and had collected a record number of Youth caps (18), and eight Under-23 caps. In spite of them, I was still overawed at being in the company of experienced campaigners such as Johnny Haynes of Fulham—an established League star while I was still at school, and who had already gained 51 caps—and Bobby Charlton, with 32 caps to his credit.

They obviously realised how I felt, and went out of their way to make me welcome.

I was soon on Christian name terms with players I had previously known only by sight, as individual members of rival First Division sides. Now we were team-mates.

Globe-Trotter

I make it part of my job as England skipper to ensure that new caps get on good social terms with the experienced internationals. As professionals they already respect each other's ability. Friendships help to create that very vital, match-winning team spirit.

It's also very important that room-mates really get on well together. I'm a fairly quiet, undemonstrative sort myself, but like a pole on a magnet I'm attracted to a person with the opposite outlook. I prefer to room with an extrovert type who's lively, full of fun and always looking on the bright side.

It's a description that fits three of my most recent "oppos"—Alan Mullery, Alan Ball and Rodney Marsh—to a "T".

That brings me to travel. If I'd been a globe-trotting millionaire, I doubt if I would have visited as many places as I have while representing England. The Moore boots have kicked a ball in over 30 countries, from America to Yugoslavia.

Climates, of course, vary a great deal. But although I've played in furnace-like heat—as in Mexico—I've never experienced the other extreme of freezing cold. The only time I've played in Russia, it was their summer. Playing in England in mid-winter is chilly enough for my blood.

Bobby Moore

talks about his career as an England International

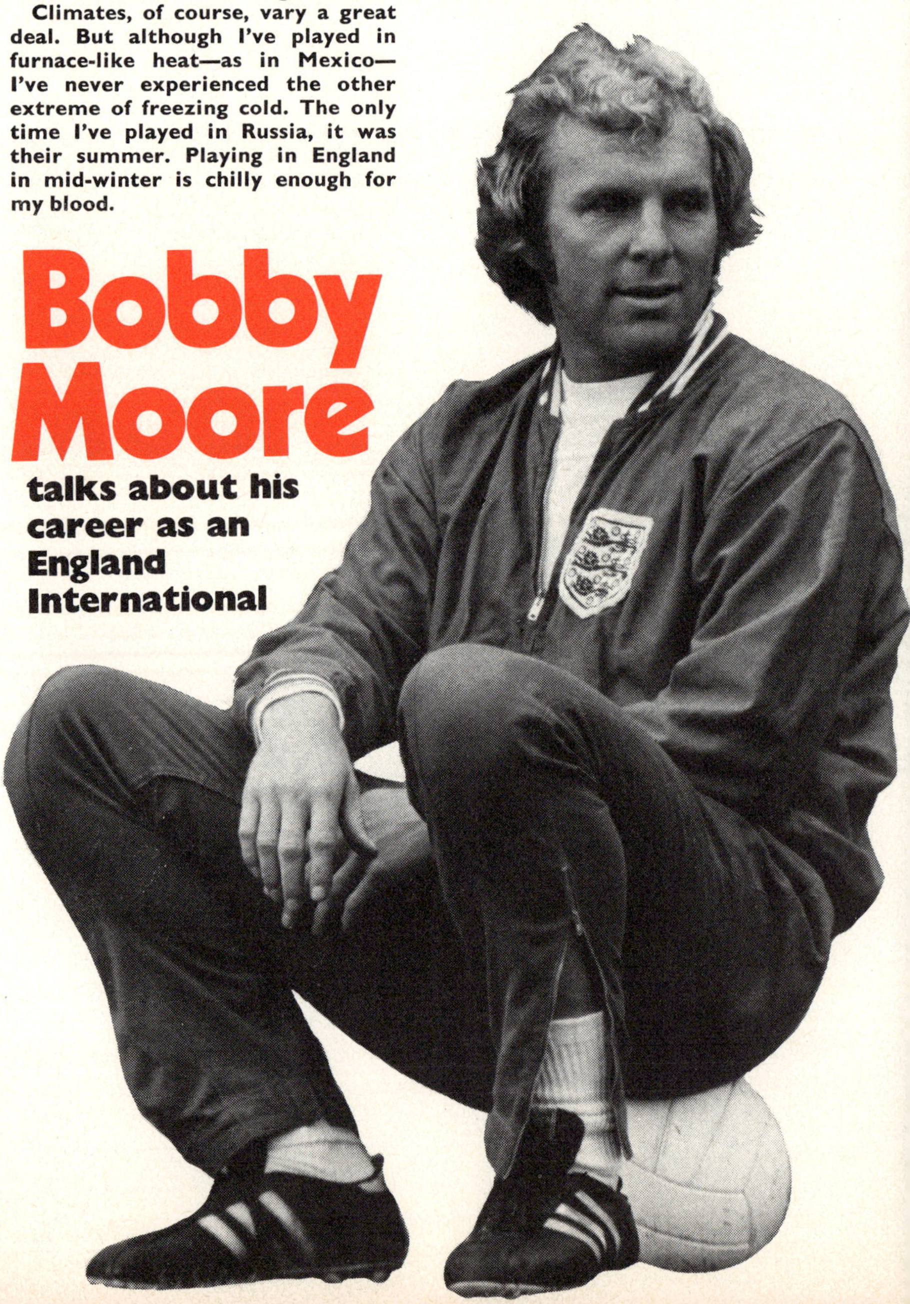

No, I must be something of a sun-worshipper, for it's the hot climes that I enjoy most. And top of the Moore places to go is Brazil. What a fabulous country!

Rio de Janeiro, the former capital city, is like a paradise. It's situated on the coast, in a bay, dominated by the world-famous Sugar Loaf Mountain and a sharp, rocky peak called The Hunchback on which stands an imposing statue of Jesus Christ, almost 100 feet high. And then there's the beautiful, golden Copaca-

ELEVEN YEARS'

bana Beach bordering the Atlantic Ocean and stretching for miles.

Cities I've visited in Eastern Europe are dull and dreary by comparison.

Strangely enough, the fans in South America and those in the Iron Curtain countries are also dissimilar. The Brazilians create a party atmosphere, with their gaily-coloured clothes, bongo drums, dancing and rhythmic singing. From before kick-off to well past full-time they maintain a deafening, ear-battering sound.

Attack!

Their opposite numbers at an Iron Curtain game watch in almost complete silence—as though viewing a game of chess—and show their appreciation of good moves by clapping their hands!

The difference in temperament between South Americans and the people of Eastern Europe is not only evident in crowd behaviour, it's also demonstrated in the way the teams play.

The Brazilian footballers are the most attack-minded in the world in my opinion. They revel in displaying their incredible ball skills, scorn defensive tactics, and go all-out for goals. Their philosophy is not to worry about how many goals they concede as long as they thump more into opponents' nets.

"Anti" Crowd

I've played against the Brazilians many times without a win. The closest we ever came to overturning them was in Guadalajara, Mexico, in the 1970 World Cup Finals.

Billed as being between the then-current World Cup holders, and the country that had won it twice before, it was the big match of the group.

I well remember leading the England side out into the blistering mid-day heat in the Jalisco Stadium. The crowd—mainly Mexican with a large scattering of Brazilians who had journeyed up by air, road and rail—were in festive mood. I was heartened to see in a far corner a welcome banner bearing a Union Jack and the words "England". Around it were clustered a band of our supporters, gallantly striving to make themselves heard above the mighty din raised by the rest of the pro-Brazil crowd.

Right from the start the Brazilians came at us, trying to overwhelm our defence with lightning passes. The great Pele—my favourite foreign player—and Tostao, a brilliant "target man", combined superbly with Jairzinho, Rivelino and Paulo Cesar to pressurise us.

We stood firm against what I consider, on its day, to be the most formidable forward line on earth. However, it wasn't all one-way traffic. We mounted several dangerous attacks and had the satisfaction of seeing our green-and-yellow shirted opponents at sixes-and-sevens.

Took Chance

Half-time came with no score. Then, 14 minutes from the re-start Tostao and Pele cleverly took out three of our men. The ball was rolled across to the nimble Jairzinho, who slotted it past the exposed Gordon Banks.

That was the only goal of a magnificent match full of end-to-end football. It was no disgrace to go down to the Brazilians, who went on

'I'll never forget the first time I played against Brazil, the most attack-minded team in international football. It was in 1962 in a World Cup Finals game. They beat us 3-1. That's me making a clearance on the right.'

to collect the World Cup trophy for the third time.

The result could have been different. Several times goal-chances came our way. As I said to a reporter afterwards: "We couldn't have come any nearer. The Brazilians made just one chance, and took it."

It's the Bulgarians who have the dubious distinction of being the most defensive side I've ever faced.

The game I'm thinking of was a World Cup Finals one, away back in 1962 in Chile.

Boring Game

We faced the Bulgars in the last match in our group. We'd collected two points from a win against Argentina, and needed at least one more point in order to qualify for the Quarter Finals. Our opponents, who had lost both their previous games, were already certain to be eliminated.

For no apparent reason, they did not attempt to attack, setting up a nine-man blanket defence which we found impossible to penetrate.

It became crystal clear they had decided to go for a draw—perhaps they couldn't face returning home with a "duck egg" as their "score"!

As our chances of getting a goal looked hopeless against such negative play, we also pulled back into defence, and settled on getting the necessary point.

The game degenerated into a sort of football "ping-pong" with the ball booted aimlessly backwards and forwards from one half to the other.

Certainly the most boring international in my career. My only consolation was that I didn't have to watch it!

No prizes for guessing when and where my most exciting experience happened. A place called Wembley—in July, 1966! The occasion: the World Cup Final between England and West Germany.

The Germans scored first through Haller. Six minutes later we equalised. I took a free kick, and Geoff Hurst headed it perfectly past Tilkowski.

Win Again!

The score stuck at 1-1 until twelve and a half minutes from the end of full-time when Martin Peters—like Geoff, a fellow West Ham teammate at the time—scored from close-in. It looked the match-winner, until the Germans were given a rather doubtful free-kick outside our area, and from it Weber equalised shortly before the final whistle.

It was then that Alf Ramsey—later to be knighted in recognition of his services to English soccer—rallied us with those now-immortal words: "You've won it once—now go out and win it again."

On the hundredth minute, Ballie—

'Although I've pulled on the England shirt over a hundred times, it's always a big thrill for me.'

Alan Ball—who almost set the turf alight with his scorching energy, crossed a ball which Hurst hit so that it cracked against the underside of the bar, bounced down—and out!

We claimed a goal—the Germans disputed it. I can still remember the tense hush as the ref consulted his linesman. The seconds seemed like hours. Then the ref pointed to the centre-spot. We *had* scored!

Almost on full-time, Geoff put the result beyond doubt, hitting a superb breakaway goal!

Great Honour

What a never-to-be-forgotten thrill it was for yours truly to receive that fabulous Jules Rimet trophy from Her Majesty Queen Elizabeth. Bobby Moore, the tubby lad from the Tom Hood Tech, Barking, the first England captain ever to grasp the most coveted Cup in football!

I won't dwell too long on the most shattering experience of my soccer life. It came almost four years later, at Leon, Mexico, in a World Cup Quarter Final. Once again we were pitted against the Germans, once again they held us to a 2-2 draw at full-time—after we had been two goals up!

"Ton-up Club"

Extra-time told a different story, though. A goal by Gerd Muller gave his country victory and revenge!

Just about the unhappiest period in my England days occurred just before those 1970 Finals, in Bogota, Colombia, after a warm-up match against that country.

After a visit to a jeweller's shop with some team-mates, I was wrongfully accused by a girl assistant of stealing a bracelet that was missing!

Although no one seriously believed I was guilty, and I was allowed to go on to Mexico to play, I felt angry and hurt at being branded a thief!

It was two years before the girl assistant was discredited and my name cleared!

On another personal note, my happiest moment came in 1973 when I became only the third man to have made over a hundred appearances for England.

The other two players to pass the magic "ton" mark are Billy Wright, capped 105 times, and Bobby Charlton, with 106 caps.

It's a real privilege to be a member of what could be called "The most exclusive club in English football"!

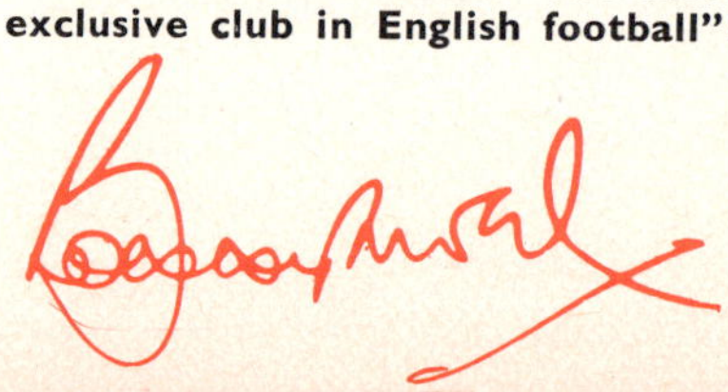

'My most exciting experience was captaining England to World Cup Final victory in 1966. Left, that's me shaking hands with Uwe Seeler, my West German opposite number. In the other photo above I'm standing next to Alan Mullery, with whom I shared a room many times as an England team-mate. Below, West Germany's Gerd Muller scores the third and decisive goal that put us out of the World Cup Finals in 1970.'

SHOOT CROSSWORD

ACROSS

1. Put money into (6)
4. Well brought up (8)
10. Celtic Scottish international defender Billy . . . (7)
11. Home ground of Southampton (3 and 4)
12. The day after today (8)
14. Leeds United Manager Don . . . (5)
16. To live in (6)
19. Mends cloth (5)
21. West Bromwich striker Jeff . . . (5)
23. A medicine (5)
28. A small glass bottle (5)
30. Southampton Manager Ted . . . (5)
31. Wedlock (8)
34. Publication (7)
35. To send out again (7)
36. Aldershot are known as . . . (3 and 5)
37. Nickname for Bill Shankly (6)

ANSWERS ON PAGE 93

DOWN

1. Inexperienced (8)
2. Hatred (5)
3. Aroused (7)
5. Obligation (4)
6. London First Division club (7)
7. Halifax are known as . . . (3 and 4)
8. To strike out (6)
9. Stoke City defender Alan . . . (5)
13. Known as the Hammers (4 and 3)
15. Notion (4)
17. Liverpool forward . . . Callaghan (3)
18. Every one (4)
20. Chelsea defender . . . Harris (3)
22. Wooden supports on railway lines (8)
24. A shot off target goes . . . (7)
25. East Anglian First-Division club (7)
26. Known as The Canaries (7)
27. Not present (6)
29. Liverpool centre-half . . . Lloyd (5)
32. Wilful setting on fire of property (5)
33. A single group (4)

GOALS ARE THEIR BUSINESS

NOTHING excites supporters like a goal—as long as it's not against their team, of course! Here, we take a colourful look at five Division One strikers whose business it is to score those fabulous goals.

LEFT: . . . Arsenal's Ray Kennedy is a young goal-grabber who is already feared amongst First Division defences . . . and he's going to get a lot better!
ABOVE . . . Bob Latchford, the bearded Birmingham front-runner, did extremely well in his first season in Division One

LEFT
Southampton's Mick Channon has made his mark at both Under-23 and full level for England. Now, the Super Saint aims to claim a regular spot in Sir Alf Ramsey's senior side.

ABOVE
Coventry City's Scottish striker Brian Alderson showed that The Sky Blues won't need to buy more strikers! He teamed up with £100,000 Colin Stein to form a deadly partnership.

ABOVE
Geoff Hurst's first season with Stoke City was, marred by a back injury. But before he was forced to rest he proved that he still had the ability to score goals in the top flight . . . something many critics doubted after his move from West Ham.

THE NIGHT MANCHESTER UNITED BECAME KINGS OF EUROPE

EUROPEAN CUP FINAL
(Wednesday May 29th, 1968, at Wembley Stadium).

Manchester Utd. (0) 4
Benfica (0) 1
(after extra-time)

Attendance 100,000
Receipts £118,000

HOW THEY LINED UP

MANCHESTER UNITED

Colours: All blue — Formation: 4-3-3

1 Stepney
2 Brennan, 5 Foulkes, 10 Sadler, 3 Dunne
4 Crerand, 9 Charlton, 6 Stiles
7 Best, 8 Kidd, 11 Aston

Substitute: Rimmer

Referee: Concetto Lo Bello (Italy)

Substitute: Naseimento

11 Simoes, 10 Eusebio, 9 Torres, 8 Augusto
7 Coluna, 6 Graca
5 Cruz, 4 Jacinto, 3 Humberto, 2 Adolfo
1 Henrique

Colours: All white — Formation: 4-2-4

BENFICA

AFTER waiting for 12 long years to reach the European Cup Final, mighty, magnificent Manchester United at last won the trophy at Wembley, on a night of anger, tension, emotion and finally glory.

It was like the 1966 World Cup Final all over again, as United, like England against West Germany, found new strength and character in a muscle-sapping period of extra-time.

But the game which ended so dramatically, so emotionally . . . started so violently. Neither team could feel proud of that foul-ridden first-half when skill and common-sense were forgotten.

The boos and shrilling whistles which greeted the players as they walked off the field after a goalless first-half, must have had some effect for there was no more trouble for referee Lo Bello.

THE ROAD TO WEMBLEY

UNITED	BENFICA
First Round	First Round
Hibernian Valletta (Malta)	Glentoran (Eire)
(h) 4-0, (a) 0-0. Won 4-0.	(h) 0-0, (a) 1-1 (won on away goals rule)
Second Round	Second Round
Sarajevo (Yugoslavia)	St. Etienne (France)
(a) 0-0, (h) 2-1. Won 2-1	(a) 1-0, (h) 2-0. Won 3-0.
Quarter-Final	Quarter-Final
Gornik Zabrze (Poland)	Vasas Budapest (Hungary)
(h) 2-0, (a) 0-1. Won 2-1.	(a) 0-0, (h) 3-0. Won 3-0.
Semi-Final	Semi-Final
Real Madrid (Spain)	Juventus (Italy)
(h) 1-0, (a) 3-3. Won 4-3.	(a) 2-0, (h) 1-0. Won 3-0.

Bobby Charlton (left) beats Benfica 'keeper Henrique with this header to score United's first goal.

The remainder of the match will forever live in the memories of all the 100,000 fans at Wembley and the estimated 20 million watching on television throughout Europe.

United began the second-half hungry for goals, and shots by John Aston worried the Benfica 'keeper Henrique.

But it was captain courageous BOBBY CHARLTON who scored first, when a cross from Dave Sadler floated near a post. The ball looked as if it was aimed too high, but there was Charlton leaping even higher to glide a header into the net.

It was all United from then on and it came as something of a surprise when the Portuguese Champions equalised with just 11 minutes to go.

The lanky, lurking figure of Torres headed the ball across United's goal-mouth for an unmarked **GRACA** to score.

That goal shattered United and their fans, and but for a fantastic save by 'keeper Alex Stepney from a Eusebio thunderbolt eight minutes later, the Cup would have been lost.

So for the first time in ten years, a European Cup Final went into extra-time.

Eight minutes after play had been restarted United broke the deadlock . . . with one of the finest goals ever seen at Wembley.

A kick by Alex Stepney found Brian Kidd, who passed to **GEORGE BEST** waiting in the centre of the field.

With an amazing display of ball control Best left four white-shirted defenders in his wake as he raced towards the Benfica goal. Then in one final act of brilliance, Best swept past 'keeper Henrique as though he were a mere shadow and flicked the ball into the net.

A couple of minutes later **BRIAN KIDD** headed the third and decisive goal for United. All hope finally faded for Benfica when **BOBBY CHARLTON** hit a fourth.

So Manchester United's dream of winning the European Cup had become a reality.

The roaring, swaying crowd cheered their heroes around Wembley. But the loudest cheer of all was reserved for the man behind their triumph . . . Matt Busby!

Above: Graca (left) slams home Benfica's equaliser with 11 minutes of full-time left. Below: Matt Busby (centre) discusses tactics with his team during the brief interval before extra-time. Bottom: Bobby Charlton's shot soars into the net for United's fourth and final goal.

MATCH FACTS AND FIGURES

UNITED		BENFICA
22	Goal Attempts	20
8	Shots Saved	8
10	Shots Off-target	11
28	Fouls	24
8	Offside	1
5	Corners	2

AFTER MATCH QUOTES

United Manager (now director) Matt Busby. "This is the most wonderful thing that has happened in my life. The boys have done me proud. They came back into this match, just as they did against Real Madrid in the Semi-Final, with a huge display of heart. I'm proud of them all."

United skipper and two goal hero Bobby Charlton. "I thought late on in the game that we had missed our best chance, and I didn't think I could pick myself up because I was so tired. But we managed it for Matt Busby."

Benfica Manager (at the time) Otto Gloria. "I do not feel very happy because to lose in the Final is not a happy moment. The trophy is in good hands because United are a very good team. But we must remember they were playing at home and this obviously was a tremendous advantage."

Benfica star Eusebio. "We are pleased for United and Matt Busby. We are very disappointed at the result, but Benfica have won the European Cup in the past. They were too strong for us in the end."

DERBY PORTRAIT GALLERY

JOHN O'HARE

KEVIN HECTOR

ARCHIE GEMMILL

JOHN McGOVERN

STEVE KINDON
(Wolves)

TOMMY HUTCHISON
(Coventry City)

FROM DIGGING COAL TO SCORING GOALS

PRESENT day transfers can often have a touch of the James Bond about them. Managers and players meet in motorway lay-byes . . . hotel rooms . . . anywhere to keep away from the ever-alert Press.

Jimmy Bone, Sheffield United's Scottish international striker, was once involved in a transfer deal that had even the newspapers beaten.

It happened when Jimmy was moving south from Partick Thistle. Ron Saunders, the Norwich City Manager, thought it might be better if Jimmy came to see him rather than vice versa.

You can't blame Ron . . . he'd have found himself in a COAL MINE!

Part-Timer

Jimmy explains the unlikely scene for the start of his career in the English Football League.

"I was only a part-timer with Thistle and worked in the Polnaise Pit.

"February 29th, 1972, was my first day back after a seven-week miners' strike.

"I arrived as usual when Davie McParland, my Thistle Manager, phoned with the news that Norwich were interested in me.

"I left work straight away. You can imagine what the lads at the pit said. Seven weeks' strike . . . and I was off again!"

Stocky Scot

Ron Saunders impressed Jimmy and the stocky Scot was happy to join The Canaries who, at the time, were in Division Two . . . but heading for Division One.

All went well as Jimmy scored four goals in 14 games—a fair rate for a player who had been only a part-timer a few weeks before.

Into Division One flew The Canaries and Jimmy had the honour of scoring the club's first goal in the top Division, against Everton.

Then . . . Norwich started to struggle as the First Division became aware of their enthusiastic style, based mostly on non-stop running and team-effort.

Jimmy was dropped and finally transferred to Sheffield United. This hurt the Scot.

"The Manager said I wasn't scoring goals. Maybe—but nobody was. It was difficult to score in a system that only used two men up front.

"When we played 4-3-3 it was easier, but in Division One it was almost impossible to score with only two strikers.

Jimmy Bone
Sheffield United

"I feel that I was made the scape-goat for the club's poor form. But it was my goals that helped them to the League Cup Final."

Wembley

Was Jimmy disappointed at missing the chance to play at Wembley?

"It's every player's dream to play there, but I hope that I can get there with Sheffield United.

"The transfer to Bramall Lane happened shortly before the Final and it took me by surprise so I didn't really have time to think about Wembley.

"I was sorry for the lads that Spurs won 1-0 . . . but I was more sorry when Arsenal beat United 3-2 the same afternoon."

Happy Year

Despite the unhappy end to his Norwich career, Jimmy says that it was a very happy year at Carrow Road.

That, however, is in the past. Norwich don't figure in Jimmy's plans any more . . . his sole aim is to reach the top with United.

The club is, at present, having its ground modernised . . . and they started to give their team a new look when they bought Jimmy from The Canaries.

Norwich may, one day, regret selling Bone . . . but one thing is certain.

There will be no more strikes for Jimmy—unless he's striking for goal, that is!

'A "FOOTBALL FIRST" I'LL NEVER FORGET'

Stars from England and Scotland recall unique moments in their thrill-filled careers.

RODNEY MARSH

My first appearance at Wembley, the home of English football, was in season 1966/67 as a Queen's Park Rangers player.

At the time, we were in the Third Division but we had fought through to the League Cup Final against West Brom, which was, incidentally, the first year the Final was at Wembley.

There was a full house that March afternoon and the atmosphere was quite unlike any other I'd experienced before.

I was only 22, but we had experienced players like Les Allen and Ron Springett to help us settle down.

We were the underdogs, of course, and few people expected us to win. Yet we went at West Brom from the kick-off and thoroughly deserved our 3-2 win.

I was lucky enough to score in our victory . . . yes, I'll never forget that first Wembley goal.

DAVID WEBB (Chelsea)

How can I ever forget my first full game in goal during a League match for Chelsea? It was on Boxing day 1971 at The Bridge against Ipswich, and I thoroughly enjoyed my experience between the sticks. I kept a clean sheet and we won 2-0.

And if I'm given the chance to play in goal again for the Chelsea first-team just try to stop me. Anyway, you never know, Sir Alf may need an emergency 'keeper some time in the near future!

LEIGHTON JAMES (Burnley)

Would you believe me if I told you that my first game for Wales was partly remembered because I played without my contact lenses!

It was in October 1971 against Czechoslovakia in a Nations Cup match in Prague.

Actually, I can't wear them under floodlights because of a certain amount of dazzle.

But I got by all right and, of course, pulling on that famous red jersey for the first time was tremendous.

Only the result disappointed me . . . Wales lost 0-1.

ALAN ROUGH (Partick Thistle)

I'll never be able to forget my first visit to Greece. Thistle played against Olympiakos in a friendly during 1971 and I've never played such a dirty team.

The Greeks kicked, punched and shoved players off the ball—luckily for me continentals seem to respect goalkeepers, but some of our outfield players came in for some rough treatment.

While we were out there, we celebrated the forthcoming weddings of Tommy Rae and John Gibson.

We started to sing and have a good time, but the waiter in our hotel misunderstood us.

He fled down the street, thinking we were going to attack him!

TREVOR FRANCIS (Birmingham)

Like all footballers, I'll always remember my first-team debut for Birmingham. It was in September 1970, and I was only sixteen years of age at the time. What's more, I scored in our side's 1-1 draw with Oxford at St. Andrews.

I'd have liked Brum to have won, of course. But netting that goal has certainly given me one of the greatest thrills of my life so far.

GRAHAM PADDON (Norwich)

The first match that stands out in my memory is a First Division game I played in for Coventry against Nottingham Forest at Highfield Road in September 1969.

With the score standing at 2-2 I nipped in to net the winner for The Sky Blues.

Playing for Norwich has given me plenty of memorable moments, of course, but on reflection I can always recall the above game.

JOE HARPER (Everton)

Although I've been with Everton for about a year, I must go back to my Aberdeen days for my magical moment. Whenever Celtic play, they are usually the favourites—one glance at their record explains why.

Yet when Aberdeen met them in the 1970 F.A. Cup Final at Hampden I was always confident of winning.

"We" did—3-1—and I collected my first major honour at the ripe old age of 22!

The highlight, though, was my penalty that clinched the game. I have a huge photograph (the one shown on the right) taken from behind the goal, in my bedroom at home.

That was a goal I shall never forget.

'A "FOOTBALL FIRST" I'LL NEVER FORGET'

Continued

EMLYN HUGHES (Liverpool)

When Sir Alf gave me the nod for England's match against Holland at Wembley in January 1970 I could have jumped over the moon. No one ever forgets his first game for England.

Unfortunately it turned out to be a disappointing evening for English fans. The score was 0-0 and we had what looked like a perfectly good goal disallowed.

DAVE WATSON (Sunderland)

Scoring goals always gives me a great kick. But my first-ever goal in League football is one I'll always remember.

It was on the 4th of October 1967 in a Fourth Division match for Notts County against Crewe at Meadow Lane.

It was the only goal of the game, too. And just to make the occasion even more memorable I was 21 on that day!

BERNARD SHAW (Sheffield Wednesday)

Although I was with Wolves for almost four years, I'll never forget my baptism in senior soccer. It was with my previous club Sheffield United in the 1962/63 season against Leyton Orient, as they were then called. It was a good game, it ended all square and I came out of it pleased with my showing.

Len Badger, who's still with The Blades of course, also made his debut in that match. In fact, we formed a new full-back partnership for Sheffield United that day.

JOHN GREIG (Rangers)

In my career with Rangers, I've had many memorable moments on the domestic scene.

Yet our European Cup-Winners' Cup victory in 1972 gave me a special thrill. I'd always wanted to skipper my only club to a European triumph . . . now, my ambition had been realised.

The Final was played in Barcelona and our opponents were Moscow Dynamo, the crack Russian team.

Thousands of our supporters had made the long trip to Spain so we felt quite at home, even though we were so far away!

We were 3-0 up, but lost concentration and allowed the Russians to make it 3-2 . . . and that's how it ended.

The only black spot was our ban from Europe the next season following the crowd scenes after our victory.

Even that couldn't cloud a lifetime ambition come true.

JIMMY JOHNSTONE (Celtic)

Season 1966/67 was the year Celtic won everything—Championship, both domestic Cups . . . and the European Cup.

I've also played on the losing side in the European Cup Final, when Dutch Champions Feyenoord beat us 2-1 in 1970. But let me tell you about that sunny afternoon in Lisbon when we beat Inter-Milan 2-1 to become the first British club to win the competition.

Half of Glasgow seemed to be in the stadium cheering us on. Inter took a dramatic lead through a penalty, but Tommy Gemmell equalised for us.

Now, those masters of defence had to play us at our own game . . . ATTACK! And we showed the world that afternoon that attack is the best form of defence.

Our forward line triumphed over the well-organised Italian defence and when Steve Chalmers hooked in the winner, millions of football fans all over Britain must have breathed with relief.

The defensive style that had made Inter famous had failed . . . Celtic, kings of attack, were also Kings of Europe!

DAVID HARVEY (Leeds)

To be honest, I didn't expect to play in the 1971 F.A. Cup Final. I'd hoped to, of course—but deep down I thought Manager Don Revie would choose the more experienced Gary Sprake to face Arsenal.

The papers were full of speculation and hinted that I might get the vote, but I didn't know until the morning of the Final that I was definitely in.

The Boss thought that I would not have slept if I'd known what was ahead—and he's probably right.

I'd had experience of an F.A. Cup Final before, when I played in the Chelsea/Leeds replay in 1970, but this was my first Wembley appearance.

What a stadium! The atmosphere was incredible, but once the game started all my nerves went.

Of course, we won 1-0 and since then I've been first-choice for Leeds.

MARTIN BUCHAN (Manchester Utd.)

No player's football education is complete until he has played in Brazil's famous Maracana Stadium.

I'll never forget my first and only appearance there against the World Champions.

It was for Scotland in the 1972 Mini World Cup. There was a huge crowd behind Brazil and our team was relatively inexperienced.

Yet for most of the game we held our own against them. Then, as it seemed as if we had earnt a draw, Jairzinho struck to rob us.

The stadium is unforgettable and I'm sure those Scots who turned down a chance of the trip missed the experience of a lifetime.

GOALS ALL THE WAY

OPPOSITE PAGE, TOP
Crystal Palace goalkeeper John Jackson dives in vain as Stoke's John .Ritchie (stripes) blasts the ball home from close range.

OPPOSITE PAGE, BOTTOM
Every footballer's dream . . . Liverpool's Peter Cormack (left) scores on his debut at Anfield. Wolves defender Frank Munro stands dejected as Peter's team-mate John Toshack raises his arms.

ABOVE
Wham! Leeds skipper Billy Bremner is airborne as he crashes home a superb goal against Derby County.

RIGHT
Newcastle United's stylish schemer Jimmy Smith jumps high above two Arsenal defenders to nod a simple goal.

BELOW
Another Merseyside debut goal! This time, it's Everton's Rod Belfitt (dark shirt, on ground) who is on the mark. The Manchester City defence is helpless as the former Leeds and Ipswich forward guides the ball past gallant goalkeeper Joe Corrigan.

'MAD KEEN' JIM WOULD PLAY FOR NOTHING!

DUNDEE'S midfield player Jimmy Wilson has seen a fair bit of soccer life. He played with Newcastle, Morton, Motherwell, and Aberdeen before moving on to Dens Park and Wilson, one of the most experienced players in Scotland, has loved every minute of it.

It is a refreshing attitude to find in today's soccer world where some players are in it purely for the money. Soccer is NOT a job to Wilson, it's a life and his skills have certainly done quite a bit to brighten the scene.

Thrives on Jeers

At the start of last season Jimmy played against his former club Motherwell three times and took a bit of stick from the Fir Park fans, but he thrived on their jeers and, in fact, looks forward to it! "I call them my fans", says Jimmy. "Whenever I play against Morton at Cappielow, Aberdeen at Pittodrie or Motherwell at Fir Park I always get a rousing reception. Maybe it's because I am only a little bloke that they think they can call me names and get away with it!

"Against Motherwell in the League match at their ground I was even being booed at the kick-in before the match. That's loyalty for you! But I answered them in the best way possible. I scored our first goal and then rushed over to the stand side with my hands held in the air as if expecting them to shower me with accolades. Of course, they burst in to a fit of jeering! I enjoyed every minute of it.

"I also remember an incident later in the game when the score stood at 2-2 and their centre-half Willie McCallum slipped while trying to clear the ball on the edge of the penalty box. It left me with a clear run at goal, but it was so unexpected that I missed the chance and the Motherwell fans actually cheered me. I would rather have them booing."

Wilson is one of the greatest characters ever to be developed in Scotland. He gets tremendous enjoyment from playing soccer and gives one the impression he would play it for nothing if he had to. In this day and age you must certainly admit that is something extra-special!

Jimmy might admit he has entered the veteran class if you pushed him enough, but his artistry won't be lost to Scottish soccer for quite some time. "Retire? Me? Could you imagine the game without me?", retorts Wilson. He has given invaluable service to all his clubs and has done a great job with Dundee and their youngsters.

Responsibility

Manager Davie White regards Wilson as a major part in his plan to bring success to Dundee and Wilson has accepted the responsibility of helping to bring on the young players. In fact, his rival for a first team place at Dens Park is Duncan Lambie and he would be the first to admit that he owes a lot to Wilson's coaching.

"Duncan is going to be a superb player," enthuses Wilson. "He is very tricky and deceptive. He is a good team man whom you know is dependable in a rigid formation."

A Joker

Wilson, the joker in the pack, has done a lot for Scottish soccer in his time and will keep on doing so. Even after he has hung up his boots for the last time his handiwork will still be there in the Dundee of tomorrow. Let's hope some of his wit has rubbed off as well. The game could do with it!

Professional football is a serious business for the players, but it can also be fun. Jimmy Wilson has surely proved that.

PETERS~The Football 'PHANTOM'

The "ghost" suddenly appeared in the penalty area from nowhere. Defenders tried desperately to grapple with him but to no avail. Skilfully eluding them, the white-shirted figure swept the ball into the net.

Yes, Martin Peters had struck again. Yet, despite his constant tally of goals the Spurs and England superstar is not a striker.

Peters became Britain's first £200,000 player when he moved to White Hart Lane from West Ham in March 1970, in an exchange deal which took the one-time idol Jimmy Greaves to Upton Park.

He later became Spurs' skipper, and England's vice-captain, and in strange keeping with his "phantom footballer" tag wears a white shirt for both club and country.

England's Manager Sir Alf Ramsey once described the quiet man of North London's famous club as being ten years ahead of his time.

"It's difficult to know exactly what Sir Alf meant by that remark but knowing him as I do I naturally took it as a compliment," says Martin.

"I believe he was suggesting that I was able to play in several different positions—something which was rare when he made the statement, but is quite commonplace now.

"Players today are able to adjust to various roles. I'm lucky in the fact that I've always been a fairly adaptable person, although if I was asked if I'd like to be an out and out striker I would have to answer 'no'.

"I think my greatest asset is that I'm able to read a game well. I seem to know exactly when to take up a good scoring position. As soon as an opening appears I 'ghost' in on the blind side of opponents and with a bit of luck score another goal for Tottenham.

"Essentially, though, I'm a midfield player. I never hold a ball too long. I try to touch it off as quickly as possible to one of my team-mates, who's probably in a better position than I am."

Peters was a member of West Ham's victorious European-Cup Winners' Cup winning side of 1965 when, in a never-to-be-forgotten fabulous feast of football, The Hammers defeated the West German side Munich 1860 by two goals to nil.

World Cup goal

But the tall, lean East Londoner really found fame the following year when as a member of the full England side he grabbed one of the four goals that helped Sir Alf's men to conquer West Germany and become the World Champions.

He didn't really hit the headlines again until his sensational move in March 1970.

How did he react to that colossal £200,000 price-tag?

"I enjoyed it," recalls the White Hart Lane skipper. "And I must confess that it was an ego-booster. It helped my play."

Two-and-a-half years later, in October 1972, the "ghost" hogged the headlines again in a way befitting one of Britain's most gifted and cultured stars. Tottenham thrashed Manchester United, George Best and all, 4-1 in a League match at Old Trafford and the majestic Martin netted all Spurs' goals.

While the Spurs skipper depicts a style of play that's almost perfection itself, the Tottenham side in general still seems to suffer through inconsistency.

"Yes, we are in-and-out," says Martin, "despite our success in Europe in recent years. If we could put our fingers on the trouble we'd romp away with the First Division title every season.

"And that's what I want more than anything else . . . a League Championship medal!"

"Last goal he scored was in 1970."

"Bit quiet on this wing, isn't it?"

LINE~UP

"Sucker."

"You being skipper doesn't allow you to kick one of your own players 'cos he missed a penalty!"

"Lovely flying header, Number 8—pity you missed the ball!"

"You always get fixed when you try that extra long throw-in!"

"I believe he's got a rather long throw."

"Old farmer Giles' bull took on something when 'ee charged our left back —"

FOR LAUGHS

"It's a wonder he doesn't score more goals with his head—it's big enough."

"That's Filpotts, our substitute—we can't afford a programme seller."

"Sliding tackle, be darned! You take that skate off your foot —"

THE HAITIAN WHOSE HEAD

One of Brazil's most famous commentators, Gerson Sabino, emerged from his trophy room in squirrel-like fashion with one of his biggest prizes—a battered old football adorned with some twenty, faded signatures. "There it is," he said proudly, "the ball used by the United States when they beat England here in Belo Horizonte; not much to look at, is she?"

Indeed she wasn't; but behind that piece of leather was a moment of football history, still, arguably, the most sensational result of all time, and certainly of the World Cup, which has enjoyed more than its fair share of sensations.

England took part in the World Cup for the first time in that year, 1950, when the Finals were held in Brazil. After beating Chile, rather laboriously, in Rio, they travelled to the mining town of Belo to take on the United States. Everyone, not least the 300 British engineers, expected England to win; any other result would have been inconceivable. That, perhaps, was the trouble; that was England's undoing.

The American team was a hotch-potch of players born, in many cases, abroad—like the centre-forward, Gaetjens, who came from the Caribbean island of Haiti; and Eddie McIlvenny, a Scotsman given a free transfer by Third Division Wrexham. Those Welsh directors must have wondered a little when they heard the result, for try as England did, they could not get the ball past McIlvenny in defence or the gallant Borghi in goal. Or, to be more precise, when they did get it past him, some leg—or arm—would turn it away, and even when Mullen's header did cross the line, it escaped the attention of the referee.

Roger Macdonald recalls some of the sensational events that have happened—on and off the field—in past World Cup Finals!

England's siege of the American goal was temporarily interrupted in the 37th minute, when a harmless cross from Bahr hit Gaetjens on the head, and sliding off in a freak manner, completely deceived Williams. That extraordinary goal proved to be the only score, with England, increasingly desperate, unable to find their way through. When the result was flashed to London by the news agencies, one by one the British newspapers sent back a query: "1-0 you say; do you mean 1-10?"

It would be pleasant to relate that the United States went on to make an impact on the competition, but, beaten by Spain and Chile, they made a speedy exit. Even Gaetjens, the Haitian whose head made history, became involved in a guerilla movement against Haiti's dictator, 'Papa' Doc, and died in a Port-au-Prince jail. The American win did little to boost the game in the United States, where it remains a summer, television spectacular, dependent on top players from abroad.

Possibly the biggest soccer sensation of all time . . . United States centre-forward Gaetjens is carried shoulder high by fans after scoring the only goal of the game to beat England 1-0 in the 1950 World Cup.

Remarkable Defeat

While England's players returned home from Rio with their tails between their legs, at least they did not have to suffer the indignities of the Italians, who in 1966, crept back into Italy at dead of night after almost as remarkable a defeat against North Korea. But even their arrival at 4.30 a.m. at Genoa Airport did not prevent some hundreds of passionate fans from surrounding the air terminal, and pelting their former heroes with stones and rotten fruit. When Italy redeemed themselves in 1970 by reaching the Final, their captain, Giacinto Facchetti, told me: "We just had to do well this time; after what happened at Genoa four years ago, we would have rather died on the field than done anything less than reached the Final."

Dedicated Team

But to give the Italians their due, the little North Koreans—not one of them was above five feet—were no scratch team hastily assembled for the occasion. On the contrary, they had been in training for two years in a remote camp in the Korean foothills, forbidden cigarettes and alcohol. Even their wives were able to visit them only once every three months. This convict-like atmosphere resulted in a dedicated team, trained to commando standards, with the kind of teamwork previously confined to the pages of Hotspur or Roy of the Rovers. If their win

MADE FOOTBALL HISTORY!

over Italy by 1-0, a goal by the quaintly named Pak Doo Ik, was helped by the serious injury to Bulgarelli, in the Quarter-Finals against Portugal, the Koreans almost achieved an even greater surprise. They actually led 3-0 before Portugal, in the shape of Eusebio, got going to run out 5-3 winners.

The score was put up progressively at Wembley, and provided welcome entertainment in view of the extraordinary hold-up during the game between England and Argentina. From the very first whistle it seemed evident that Antonio Rattin, the towering Argentine captain, intended to have more than his say in the running of the game; but eventually he went too far, and the West German referee, little Rudolf Kreitlein, sent him off for what amounted to insolence. At least he tried to send him off; it took the combined efforts of Kreitlein, the FIFA representative at the match, Ken Aston, several Argentine officials and three patient London policemen to get him moving in the direction of the tunnel. In all the game was held up for nearly ten minutes, before Argentina resumed with ten men. In retrospect, it was perhaps fortunate for England that they achieved a numerical advantage; because

The Diddy Men celebrate! The tiny North Koreans show their feelings after their victory over Italy in the 1966 World Cup Finals. Not one of the Koreans was over five feet high!

It's the Koreans again! Yong Sung Kook heads their third goal against mighty Portugal in the 1966 World Cup. Eusebio took over then—and Portugal won 5-3.

they made heavy weather of victory, a glancing header from Geoff Hurst finally beating Roma in the last quarter of an hour.

Roberto Perfumo, one of Argentina's defenders, told me some time later that all Rattin's colleagues had been astonished, not to say a little embarrassed, by his conduct on the field. "It wasn't at all typical," said Perfumo. "Rattin did not behave that way in South America at all. I can only think that the occasion, the tension, was too much for him, and he lost his head."

Cold Fury

In Argentina, of course, the news of Rattin's dismissal and their team's defeat was received with cold fury. Sir Alf Ramsey's description of their team as "animals" was widely quoted, and the picture of him preventing Cohen from exchanging shirts with an Argentinian at the end of the match was splashed across the front pages. There were even suggestions that West Germany and England had rigged the Quarter-Finals, because an English referee sent off two Uruguayans on the same afternoon in an even more violent match that had been overshadowed by the affair at Wembley. Uruguay lost 4-0, but photographs showed subsequently that the West German full-back, Schnellinger, handled the ball on the line beyond any question of doubt before a goal had been scored.

The most distasteful moment of the '66 World Cup. Argentina captain Rattin (centre) refuses to leave the field after being sent off. The game was held up for 10 minutes.

An English referee, Arthur Ellis, was also in charge of perhaps the most sensational post-war match between European and South American sides, the so-called "Battle of Berne", in 1954, when Switzerland were the host nation. In the Quarter-Finals Hungary beat Brazil 4-2, but not before three players had been sent off. First to go were Nilton Santos and Bozsik, after a boxing match in midfield, then Tozzi, another Brazilian, for kicking an opponent. But hostilities did not stop at the final whistle. After police had escorted both teams to their respective dressing-rooms, and breathed a huge sigh of relief, the lights in the underground passages suddenly went out, and the Hungarians were attacked by the entire Brazilian team, who had made, or taken advantage of, the opportunity. It was nearly 20 minutes before order was restored, when the Hungarian dressing-room resembled a casualty station in battle, with groaning players—from both teams—receiving first aid.

Gang Warfare

Yet by all accounts, the occasion was little more than a damp squib compared to the "Battle of Bordeaux" in the 1938 World Cup in France, a game that became little more than an example of gang warfare. Brazil, again, were involved, this time with Czechoslovakia, who throughout the match made no concessions to the Latin dislike of hard tackling. The affray began soon after the start when Zeze, caught in possession by Nejedly, retaliated with such violence that he was dispatched to the dressing-rooms by the Hungarian referee, Hertza. Zeze was followed, close on half-time, by Machados and the Czech winger Riha, who swapped punches on the touchline, oblivious of the position of the ball, and of the approaching referee. Six minutes had to be added on to the first half because of injuries, which by the end of the match included three hospital cases—Planicka, the Czech goalkeeper, with a broken arm; Nejedly, with a broken right leg; and Kostalek, with a painful stomach injury. The result was a 1-1 draw, and the extent of the casualty list could be seen 48 hours later, when the tie was resumed. Brazil won 2-1,

English referee Jim Finney tries to restore law and order after he had sent off a Uruguayan player in the 1966 World Cup game against West Germany at Hillsborough.

fielding nine new players, the Czechs six.

Curiously enough, Brazil also took part in a match against Poland in 1938 that made the headlines for entirely different reasons—the number of goals scored. It ended in a 6-5 victory for the Brazilians, but only after extra time, and only after a player on each side, Brazil's Leonidas and Willimowski of Poland, had each scored four goals—a record in itself. Leonidas, the "Black Diamond", astonished the crowd by demonstrating the acrobatic "bicycle kick", never before seen in Europe. In the second half, with the mud in the Strasbourg stadium slowing him down, he took his boots off and threw them to the touchline—but the Swedish referee, Eklind, said it was against the rules, and made him put them on again.

Flood of Goals

There was scarcely a game to equal it until the 1970 World Cup, when Italy met West Germany in the Semi-Finals. Italy led for much of the match, only for the Germans to equalise on the stroke of ordinary time. Playing at altitude, both teams were close to collapse, and with both defences wide open, goals came in a veritable flood. First Germany went ahead with a touch from Muller that staggered over the line with Poletti and Albertosi scrambling in pursuit, Italy equalised and went ahead, then Muller headed in for 3-3, before Rivera finally scored the winner. But with five goals in extra time, the European reporters desperately dictated their stories over open lines back home, where it was fast approaching one o'clock in the morning. And when the final whistle went amid a tumultuous din, it was anyone's guess whether the Press or the players were the more exhausted . . . .

The 1970 World Cup Semi-Final between Italy and West Germany produced seven goals. Here, Luigi Riva (right) fires home Italy's third goal as Schnellinger (left) looks on.

JOHN MARSH
Stoke

Liverpool superstar KEVIN KEEGAN reveals how he broke into the soccer big time . . .

'FIVE MINUTES LATE–AND I WENT FROM THE FOURTH DIVISION TO THE FIRST!'

Kevin was astonished when he caught his first glimpse of The Kop filled with 26,000 wildly enthusiastic Liverpool fans.

I'M a man who prides himself on being punctual—and yet if I hadn't been late on one particular occasion I'd possibly be playing in the Fourth Division now!

It happened like this: I was a youngster of about 15 at the time, and mad keen to make a career in football, so I was pleased when I was invited along for a night training session with Doncaster Rovers, my local team.

Unfortunately, though, I was delayed on my journey to the ground, and when I arrived five minutes late everybody had gone off somewhere.

And that was that. Rovers didn't contact me again. It was another false start to my career. Previously I was with Coventry City on schoolboy forms, but there didn't seem to be any future for me with

Kevin Keegan proudly displays SHOOT'S Most Exciting English Player Trophy, which he received in 1972.

Ray Clemence . . . like Keegan, he played for Scunthorpe before joining Liverpool.

them and eventually the whole thing fizzled out.

But fortunately I later got my chance with Scunthorpe. I joined them when I was 16 and got into the first-team after about eight months.

My League debut was in an away match at Peterborough, and I didn't even know I was playing until we got down there. I thought the lads were pulling my leg when they said I was in the team!

Ron Ashman, Scunthorpe's Manager at the time, just told me to go out and enjoy myself. "Play it simple," he said. I did —and I hardly had a kick!

I'd been playing in midfield for the reserves, but as an inexperienced youngster I couldn't be expected to fill that important role in the first-team, so I came in as a winger.

At that time I didn't have the confidence to take on opponents. When I got the ball I just passed it. I didn't do anything individually creative and felt I was absolutely of no use to the team at all.

As for the match itself, Peterborough were a good side, but with about ten minutes to go we were leading 2-1. Then the opposition went and scored twice to win 3-2.

A disappointing start then, but I kept my place and after a few games the confidence started to come. And when I had about ten matches under my belt I had settled down.

I still wasn't happy playing on the wing, however, but someone else's misfortune proved my lucky break. A player was injured, I was moved back to replace him in midfield, and I really savoured the freedom. I'd felt tied down as a winger.

From there on I thoroughly enjoyed myself at Scunthorpe. I was on top money and thought I was playing pretty well.

We had a good side and there were always stories that scouts from the big clubs were watching us.

At one time it looked as if I was set to join Arsenal and naturally I was delighted at the prospect of going to such a glamorous club.

But I changed my opinion when Ron Ashman called me into his office and said The Gunners wanted to take me on a youth tour to look me over before deciding whether to sign me.

Mr. Ashman had my best interests at heart, but the way I saw it Arsenal had to take me or leave me as I was. I wasn't keen to go abroad with the young lads because, after all, I was a full-time footballer then playing regularly in the League.

But as it turned out I didn't have to make the final decision on whether to accept Arsenal's offer. The F.A. refused permission for me to go on the Highbury club's tour because I wasn't officially one of their players.

Now, I feel very pleased I couldn't go because I've ended up with Liverpool, the best club in the country.

I wasn't sure of my prospects when Bill Shankly put in a bid for me, though. I'd seen Liverpool play on television, and while I had faith in my ability, I wasn't certain I could make the grade at Anfield.

But finally I talked it over with my dad and decided I had nothing to lose by accepting the challenge. I reasoned that if things didn't work out at Liverpool, I could still move into a lower Division.

So I went to Anfield for a fee of £33,000, and to be honest I wasn't that happy at first.

I joined Liverpool on the Monday before they met Arsenal in the 1971 F.A. Cup Final and in the beginning I thought nobody wanted to know me. It was only later that I realised everyone was too wrapped up in the forthcoming Wembley occasion.

At the start I didn't enjoy my football with Liverpool very much either. I was in the reserves, playing in midfield, and as I didn't know the style of the players around me I kept pushing the ball about and losing it.

In a nutshell, I was struggling.

Moved forward

Then came a change for the better. I was used as a front-runner in a reserve game against Southport and got two goals.

That brought me promotion to the first-team for our 1971 close-season tour in Sweden.

Operating as a striker was like a weight off my shoulders. I wouldn't want to play in midfield again because you can't afford to give a ball away there. One mistake can cost a goal.

I was pleased when I moved from the wing with Scunthorpe, but I was even happier about my change of position with The Reds.

Despite the improvement in my fortunes, I still didn't reckon I'd proved myself. It was only when I made my League debut, against Nottingham Forest at Anfield in the opening game of the 1971-72 season, that I really felt a part of the first-team.

Bill Shankly (above) paid Scunthorpe £33,000 for Keegan. Below: 'Pool goalkeeper Ray Clemence saves from Arsenal's George Armstrong (light shirt) in the 1971 F.A. Cup Final.

That match is one I'll never forget, but at one stage I thought I was going to miss it! Being, as I said earlier, a punctual type, I left early for the ground, but the size of the crowd making their way to the stadium astonished me.

I got stuck in a bumper-to-bumper traffic jam in my car and didn't think I was going to reach the ground in time. Luckily, I did, though.

But when we ran out on to the pitch there was another shock. I just couldn't stop looking at The Kop. I'd seen it empty, obviously, but the sight of it crammed with a heaving mass of 26,000 chanting fans was almost unbelievable.

When the match got under way, I was conscious of the faster pace in Division One, but all the same I found it easier than playing with Scunthorpe because I had better players around me.

The game with Forest had a happy start and a happy ending for me. I scored after only twelve minutes, but I'll admit there was an element of luck about it. I tried to crash the ball home but mis-hit it and it screwed into the corner of the net.

Funnily enough, I possibly wouldn't have scored otherwise. If I'd connected properly the goalkeeper would have anticipated the direction.

The happy ending came with the final score, of course. We beat Forest 3-1.

That was the start of the big-time for yours truly. And now as I look ahead I foresee many wonderful years with this great Liverpool club.

No disrespect to Doncaster Rovers, but I'm glad now that I was too late for their training session!

Kevin Keegan

SCORE-LINE

Corner	66 N	10 F	2 L	15 B	7 J	3 V	✱
56 K	36 P	8 E	6 X	5 U	1 P	8 O	11 G
9 G	2 D	1 C	4 Z	14 O	16 W	22 D	2 K
20 W	22 T	24 F	26 V	3 L	10 A	19 B	4 P
10 U	12 T	6 D	30 C	1 S	12 J	18 E	3 Y
4 J	2 O	3 M	36 K	2 W	8 G	20 L	16 I
14 L	28 B	34 F	32 X	5 D	16 V	8 R	5 Z
✱	12 D	18 K	9 F	6 G	30 P	15 H	GOAL

THE answer to each of the questions below is a number. Starting at the "Corner" join each of the squares (by their centre dots) which contain these numbers. The squares must be adjoining—down, across or diagonally—and used once only. Thus you will find a route to goal. If you have joined the correct squares the letters in them are also the jumbled name of an English First Division club.

1) England won the World Cup in 19— [66].
2) The crossbar of a soccer goal is — [8] feet from the ground.
3) Celtic are in Division — [1] of the Scottish Football League.
4) The number of clubs in the English First Division. [22]
5) The penalty spot is — [12] yards from the goal-line.
6) The number of goals in a "hat-trick". [3]
7) The very first World Cup Competition was held Uruguay in 19— [30].
8) The number of goals scored in the 1972 F.A. Cup Final (Leeds v Arsenal). [1]
9) During the taking of a free kick the opponents must stand at least — [10] yards from the ball.
10) The number of clubs in the Scottish First Division. [18]
11) Aston Villa were top of the English Division — [3] at the end of the 1971/2 season.
12) The weight of the soccer ball should not exceed — [16] ounces.
13) The number of teams left in a knock-out competition at the Quarter-Finals stage. [8]
14) The number of minutes in each half of normal "extra time". [15]

MANCHESTER CITY

ANSWER ON PAGE 40

THEY SERVE THE STRIKERS

BELOW . . . Two London stars who made their mark last season . . . West Ham's Pat Holland and John Pratt of Tottenham Hotspur (white shirt). Pat got his chance when Bryan Robson was moved back into the firing line, and it is more than a coincidence that Bryan scored a hatful of goals. Young Pat gave him great service from midfield. John took over the number four shirt at Spurs when Alan Mullery was transferred to Fulham. He is a worthy successor to the former England star.

ABOVE . . . . Norwich City's Welsh international Trevor Hockey (seen in the colours of his former club, Sheffield United) is now showing all his old enthusiasm and fire.

BELOW . . . Doug Livermore, one of the Norwich stars who helped The Canaries to a place in last term's League Cup Final.

ABOVE
Two of Division One's outstanding schemers—Asa Hartford of West Brom and Chelsea's John Hollins (blue strip).
TOP RIGHT
Wolves midfield man Kenny Hibbitt has a very promising future.
RIGHT
Leeds United and Eire general Johnny Giles, a world-class player.

Ian Callaghan, the "old man" of the Liverpool team, was perhaps The Reds' most consistent player last season.

'I GOT NOWHERE WITH NON-STOP RUNNING'

by Wolves striker JOHN RICHARDS

WHEN John Richards exploded into the Wolves team, he was lucky to play alongside an experienced professional such as Derek Dougan.

After a few occasional appearances, John finally made his mark in 1971/72 with 13 League goals from 35 outings.

His partner, The Doog, grabbed 15 and played possibly the best football of his career.

Coincidence? Over to Johnny Giles, the Leeds and Eire schemer.

"Although Derek has obviously helped John, I'd say that John also gave Derek a lot of aid.

"John takes a lot of weight off Derek and provides him with some delightful nod-downs or short passes in the penalty-area.

Late Starter

"At 33, I'd say Derek was given a new lease of life by the arrival of young Richards, who I'm sure is booked for a long career with England."

John, himself, is modest about the effect he had on Dougan and praises the Irishman for his help and encouragement.

"Derek had a world-wide reputation, and when I came into the side I was unknown. Defenders used to watch him and his unselfish running enabled me to score a few goals."

Now, John grabs his goals as if they were going out of fashion. He was the club's leading scorer last season and became a regular in the Under-23 side.

The Wolves sharpshooter was a "late starter"—he didn't sign professional terms until he was 18. How has he changed during these four years?

"I used to run . . . and run . . . and run—but got nowhere. I wasn't using my energy properly.

"Manager Bill McGarry and his assistant Sammy Chung spent a lot of time teaching me where to run and when to do it. They impressed upon me that it was no use dashing around without doing the right things.

"They taught me decoy runs, how to hold the ball . . . they polished my rough edges.

"I used to watch Geoff Hurst and admire him for his ability on and off the ball. He shields it so well from opponents and his reading of the game amazed me."

One Fault

But how far is Richards from making the sort of mark the former England striker made?

Says McGarry: "John still lacks a little bit of confidence. He's scored a lot of goals but he could have had even more.

"He works himself into scoring positions yet sometimes fluffs the chances. Once he conquers this—and I'm sure it won't be long—John will be an outstanding player."

As McGarry is not noted for talking about his players' qualities, this can be taken as quite a compliment.

Perhaps Richards' greatest asset is that he always looks as if he is likely to score. He has that goal-hungry look about him that makes the difference between a good striker and a great one.

John is so fast off the mark that it takes a nippy defender to even keep up with him. If John's given a yard start, it can be fatal to the opposition.

Wolves have a tradition of attacking football and this is certainly being carried on by Richards the First.

SCORELINE ANSWERS

1) 66, 2) 8, 3) 1, 4) 22, 5) 12, 6) 3, 7) 30, 8) 1, 9) 10, 10) 18, 11) 3, 12) 16, 13) 8, 14) 15.
"MANCHESTER CITY"

'BURNLEY ARE GOING PLACES'

says Keith Newton

BURNLEY'S displays in the Second Division last season were a revelation. The club, with a squad of young players, played some of their best football ever.

One player who stood out amongst Manager Jimmy Adamson's exciting side in 1972-73 was left-back Keith Newton.

At 32 years of age he's the "old man" of the Turf Moor team. Does the veteran tag bother him at all?

"Veteran—me? You must be joking. Mind you, I think a lot of people got the impression I'd drifted in to the backwaters of soccer when Everton gave me a free transfer over a year ago and I ended up joining Burnley.

Mexico Success

"But my move was like a breath of fresh air. I was no longer regarded as a member of the first-team squad at Goodison Park so the time had come for me to break away. And when Burnley stepped in for my signature I saw it as a great chance to add a bit of my experience to a mainly young side."

Experience was probably the key factor missing in a team made up mostly of fresh-faced youngsters who would run forever but often didn't know exactly when to slow things down.

Yes, Keith Newton has been around, all right. Before his days at Everton he was with Blackburn Rovers where he signed professional forms in October, 1960.

He started out as a wing-half but was eventually converted to a full-back and later developed into one of England's finest defenders.

So it was no surprise when Sir Alf Ramsey drafted Newton into the England squad, and in February 1966 classy Keith won his first full cap for the men in white—the match being at Wembley against West Germany.

Twenty-six more caps followed before the swashbuckling Newton was dropped from the England set-up following their ill-fated 1970 World Cup campaign in Mexico. Keith, incidentally, played in three of England's four matches and emerged as one of Ramsey's few successes in that competition.

By then Newton had changed clubs, having signed for mighty Everton in December 1969 for £80,000, after making over 300 first-team appearances for Blackburn Rovers.

Did Burnley's commanding full-back miss the atmosphere of a big-time club like Everton?

"Yes and no," replied Keith. "I miss all the big gates I used to play in front of at Goodison Park, but what people still don't seem to realise is the population of Burnley and the surrounding districts is small compared with a place like Liverpool.

"But I'll tell you this. Our fans are a grand bunch and the facilities at Turf Moor are a lot better than people would imagine."

One other fact that was obvious to our SHOOT reporter is that Keith is enjoying himself these days, perhaps more than he's ever done.

"Yes, I revel in playing for Burnley," enthused Keith. "It's a club that's going places—and I only hope that I'll still be around to help them!"

THEIR FAME SPANS THE WORLD

THE 1974 World Cup is only months away now and the prospect of seeing the top continental stars in action again thrills all fans. The 1970 tournament was fabulous . . . but, you never know, the next one could be even better. Here are a few of the players who could be on parade.

FAR LEFT . . . Probably the most gifted midfield player in the world, the incomparable Gunter Netzer of host nation West Germany. **LEFT . . .** Holland and Ajax captain Johan Cruyff is still in his mid-twenties, but already he is an established household name. **ABOVE . . .** Balint (left) of Hungary and Belgium's Dockx seen in a Nations Cup tie last year. **RIGHT . . .** Russian defender Kurtislava hopes to be on view in West Germany. **BELOW . . .** Tostao (centre), in action against Portugal, will probably lead Brazil's attack again next year.

IN ten years' time I hope to be the Manager of a successful club. Football is in my blood and it's the only job I ever want.

When I'm sitting comfortably in my "hot seat" I shall be able to look back on a career that has given me just about everything.

I've collected some wonderful memories to date . . . and rather than wait until I hang up my white boots, I'd like to talk about some of the outstanding games I've played in so far.

Like every professional, I'll never forget my League debut. Of course, I was a Blackpool player at the time, standing little over five feet and not weighing very much either!

A debut is always special, but mine was EXTRA special. Why? I made my introduction to the big-time of the Football League at Anfield, home of mighty Liverpool.

Could there be a more nerve-tingling ground for an untried teenager to receive his baptism?

Funnily enough, I wasn't too nervous, but as kick-off time approached the butterflies crept up on me.

ALAN BALL TALKS ABOUT HIS GREAT GAMES

'MY SURPRISE HAT-TRICK OF CAPS'

You see, I wasn't really expected to play well, so I had everything to gain and little to lose.

A good pass was made to seem great and a bad ball . . . well, such a young lad could be forgiven.

At least, that was the attitude of the Press, but I was well satisfied with my performance and especially the result: Liverpool 1, Blackpool 2.

My first taste of international football came in 1964 against Wales.

This was also the first occasion a Manager had instructed me to play in a specific way. Previously, I'd been given a lot of freedom.

No Promises

Against Wales, however, Sir Alf Ramsey told me to play as an "old fashioned" inside-right, coming deep and supplying winger Johnny Sissons (now Sheffield Wednesday) with passes.

England won the game 3-2, so I like to think I played my part in the victory.

After the game, Alf told me I'd done well . . . but made no promises about future selection.

In all, I won eight Under-23 caps, scoring two goals. Once I had a taste of football at this level, I wanted a full cap.

This eventually came on a close-season tour in 1965, a year before the World Cup was due to be played in England.

I went on the tour hoping to get a run-out in one game, so you can imagine how I felt when I came home with three caps—and one goal!

My England debut was in the 1-1 draw against Yugoslavia in Belgrade.

But the outstanding moment of the tour was when I scored my first England goal against Sweden in the closing match.

The pitch was greasy through rain and as the ball came through a defender missed his interception . . . which made scoring a lot easier for yours truly!

Luckily, I've collected enough England caps to fill a fairly large cabinet, but THE biggest thrill of all was winning the 1966 World Cup.

I must tell you of a funny story that happened BEFORE the game. The England party was staying in the Hendon Hall Hotel and it seemed as if everybody in the country knew who we were . . . except an American lady in the same hotel.

During our time there, we often passed the time of day with her.

On the morning of the Final, we were preparing to leave when she said: "Oh boys, where are you going? Aren't you going

"In the 1966 World Cup Final, West Germany took an early lead, but this Geoff Hurst header soon put us on level terms."

"My second F.A. Cup loser's Medal . . . Leeds beat Arsenal 1-0 in 1972. This picture shows Leeds' skipper Billy Bremner and Charlie George (red shirt) in action."

to watch the big match on the television?"

Little did she realise it, but the lady did us a favour. We were all feeling on edge and this remark helped to ease the tension.

The Final itself against West Germany was not the most exciting of the tournament, but it was the most vital.

Alf gave me a roving commission and we thought the German weakness in defence was Karl Schnellinger. It was hoped that I could exploit his lack of pace.

I kept at him whenever I could and eventually the defence cracked under the strain.

Mind you, they gave us an early fright. Left-back Ray Wilson made just about his only mistake of the entire competition and presented Haller with a goal.

We weren't too downhearted. We knew we had it in us to fight back.

Bobby Moore flighted an inch-perfect free-kick to Geoff Hurst and we equalised.

When Martin Peters capitalised on a bad clearance to make it 2-1 I thought we were home and dry.

However, the Germans possess the same fighting spirit as ourselves and with only seconds left to go, Weber scrambled the ball home to level the scores.

Disputed Goal

If you can imagine how you would feel if you'd lost £100 and found a penny, you'll begin to realise how we felt at that moment.

Alf was magnificent then. He calmly told us that we'd won the Final once . . . now we had to win it again.

There we were, wanting the grass to swallow us up—and Alf revived our spirits with one sentence. No wonder he's the best Manager England have ever had!

In extra-time came the goal that will be talked about as long as football is played. Remember it?

Geoff Hurst blasted the ball into the top of the German goalmouth . . . it hit the crossbar and bounced out.

Roger Hunt was a few yards away from the incident and could have made double sure of the goal. But he was so certain that the ball WAS in that he immediately turned to congratulate Geoff.

I have the utmost respect for Roger as a professional and the former Liverpool striker would not have walked away if there had been even the slightest doubt in his mind that the ball hadn't gone over the line.

The referee was not positioned properly to judge for himself, so he consulted his linesman.

The linesman was not up with play and in my view could not possibly have been 100 per cent certain what had happened, but he said it was a goal.

If I had been a German I would have felt a little cheated.

We secured the Final with a well-taken fourth goal by Geoff Hurst, so the disputed goal did not decide the outcome . . . I'm pleased to say.

The Germans had their revenge four years later when they beat us 3-2 in the Mexico World Cup.

With the next World Cup only a matter of months away, Colin Bell and Norman Hunter.

I thought these moves were correct. They were designed to help us hold our lead and the fact that we lost it was due to the players, not the Manager.

It's so unlike England to toss away a two-goal lead . . . but we've learnt from this mistake, I can assure you.

Another international that gave me a great deal of satisfaction was the 1972 game against Scotland at Hampden Park.

Their Manager at the time, Tommy Docherty, is not an admirer of mine, and said so publicly before the clash.

These remarks made me even more keen to show him time they went wide.

Then, Jeff Astle had all the luck in the world when a shot rebounded on to his favourite left foot and his second try gave goal-keeper Gordon West no chance.

In 1972, I was back at Wembley for another F.A. Cup Final . . . Arsenal against Leeds.

This was a very close game and it became obvious that whoever scored first would win.

I was a leg away from getting that goal! The ball came over from a corner on the left and I met it perfectly on the volley.

It screamed towards the Leeds goal with 'keeper David Harvey helpless.

My hands were raised and I

"Before the 1972 Scotland/England game, the Scots' Manager at the time, Tommy Docherty, said some unkind things about me. It gave me great pleasure to score the only goal of the game—here you see Martin Chivers following through with 'keeper Bobby Clark well beaten."

fans still talk about this match.

We were leading 2-0 and seemed booked for a place in the Semi-Finals.

Then . . . Beckenbauer fired home a long-range effort to reduce the arrears.

Uwe Seeler headed an equaliser and once again we had to play extra-time.

This was the occasion when Gerd Muller first became known to English supporters. I wish that he had waited . . . he scooped the winner to put Germany in the last four.

Some people blamed goalkeeper Bonetti. Others said Alf made the wrong substitutions, when he took off Bobby Charlton and Martin Peters for what I could do and when I scored the only goal of the game I was absolutely delighted.

Even then, Tommy insisted that it was "a comical goal." I bet he would have settled for victory by a "joke" goal!

I appeared once at Wembley with Everton, in an F.A. Cup Final—and it was a disaster.

This was in 1968 when West Brom beat us 1-0. We had one of those frustrating afternoons when nothing would go right for us.

Moves and passes that had worked in the League went astray. I had a couple of good scoring chances that I would normally have gobbled up. This was about to shout "GOAL" . . . when Paul Reaney stuck out a leg to deflect my shot.

I felt sick. Looking back, it seems obvious that after this failure Leeds were destined to take the Cup for the first time in their history.

Allan Clarke did this with a flying header . . . and that was that.

My biggest ambition now is to help Arsenal win the European Cup. I've a feeling that one day soon I'll be able to tell you about how this wish came true.

A team died so they could be born. They lost their first match. They struggled against falling gates. Today they are one of the world's leading clubs. They are . . .

MANCHESTER CITY

Billy Meredith (top of page, left) was as famous in his era as Francis Lee (above) is today. Another Manchester City (right) hero from the past . . . the great Frank Swift.

MAKING soccer history is nothing new for Manchester City . . . they've been doing that down through the years. But there is one page of history they would like to forget . . . the time they became the only club in the Football League to end a season as top-scorers in the First Division and get relegated.

It happened in 1937-38 when they scored 80 goals—three more than Arsenal who won the League Championship!

Although City found it easy scoring goals, League points were harder to get. They managed only 36 and down they went—just a year after winning the League title.

In recent seasons Manchester City have established themselves as one of Britain's most successful clubs of all time. Their name is known and respected throughout the soccer world.

Their players are among the best anywhere . . . their exciting and highly-entertaining brand of football thrills millions in a season . . . their ideas and methods are copied by clubs hoping for similar success. But it wasn't always like that!

Left: City 'keeper Bert Trautmann dives at the feet of Birmingham forward Peter Murphy during the 1956 F.A. Cup Final. As a result of this collision Trautmann broke his neck. Below: Don Revie . . . responsible for the plan that reshaped the game in Britain.

Indeed, as with many of today's top clubs, their beginnings were complicated and humble.

Manchester City were born as far back as 1880 when a team called West Gorton St. Marks played on the Kirksmanshulme cricket ground. Later they joined forces with West Gorton Athletic—called themselves simply Gorton—and struggled to survive.

Then in 1887, the club rented a piece of land from the railway and decided on a new name . . . Ardwick.

By 1892 the club had joined the newly-formed Second Division. But despite a fairly successful period in the League, lack of support and funds forced Ardwick into extinction.

Ardwick died, but their spirit was still very much alive and out of the ruins rose a new club . . . Manchester City!

The reformed club were allowed to keep the Second Division place vacated by Ardwick—despite the fact, that at the time, City had no players on their books!

But men were found and a team was brought together and they were ready to do battle. Manchester City's first League match took place on 1st September, 1894 . . . and they lost to Bury.

First Honour

It soon became apparent that City's attack would have to be strengthened. So a few weeks later a young Welshman named Billy Meredith was given the chance to prove himself.

Meredith was an immediate success. His drive and power from the wing helped the club rise to glory.

The Welshman who became as famous for City as today's stars Colin Bell, Francis Lee and Rodney Marsh, guided the club to promotion in 1889, and he scored the goal which won the F.A. Cup in 1904.

That Cup triumph against Bolton was City's first major trophy—it was also to be their last for some 30 years.

Billy Meredith—capped 51 times for Wales—played his last game for City in an F.A. Cup Semi-Final against Newcastle United on 29th March, 1924, just four months short of his 50th birthday.

With Meredith gone, some of the spark seemed to be missing from City and two years later they were relegated. They reached the F.A. Cup Final the same season, but were, ironically, beaten 1-0 by . . . Bolton Wanderers.

New Era

However, with the approaching 1930's came the beginning of a new era at Maine Road—the ground they had moved to seven years earlier.

City won back their First Division status in 1927-28 when they scored 100 goals and gained 59 points. They finished third in 1929-30 (91 goals 47 points).

In 1933 they again reached the F.A. Cup Final, only to lose 3-0 to Everton. However, the next season they were back at Wembley and beat Portsmouth 2-1.

Three years later—in the 1936-37 season—City scored 107 goals and won the League Championship—an achievement they didn't repeat until the Mercer/Allison days in 1968. One of the teams relegated that 1936-37 season were—and whisper this around Old Trafford—Manchester United.

But amazingly, a year after that memorable triumph came despair. City, despite scoring those 80 historic goals, were relegated, along with West Bromwich Albion, to the Second Division.

Disastrous

One thing made that season even more disastrous for City. Up from Division Two—and whisper this around Maine Road—came arch rivals Manchester United.

However, with the resumption of League football after the Second World War, Manchester City returned to the First Division with Burnley (1946-47), slipped back three years later, and won promotion in 1950-51 as runners-up to Preston.

City's Manager in those days was their former centre-half Les McDowell, who was the man responsible for the introduction of a tactical move which was to reshape the game in Britain.

Known as The Revie Plan—after Don Revie who later found more fame and success as the Manager of Leeds United—it was basically this: lying deep, the centre-forward (Revie) sprayed passes to his wingers. He controlled the middle of the field, in a similar role to the midfield men of today.

Cup Heroes

Using the Revie Plan, Les McDowell guided Manchester City to the F.A. Cup in successive seasons. In 1955 they lost 3-1 to Newcastle United after their full-back Jimmy Meadows (who had won his first England cap a week before) had been carried off seriously injured.

Jimmy never played again, but City were back at Wembley the following season when they defeated Birmingham City 3-1.

Don Revie was the brilliant inspiration of this victory, but we must not forget those other heroes . . . Roy Paul, Roy Clarke, Dave Ewing, Bill Leivers, Little, Barnes, Hayes, Dyson and Bobby Johnstone—the first player to score in a Wembley Cup Final two seasons in succession.

Above: Malcolm Allison, Tony Book (centre) and Joe Mercer (right) celebrate winning the League Cup in March 1970. Right: A few weeks later, Manchester City beat Gornik Zabrze in Vienna to win the European Cup-Winners' Cup. Here Neil Young (stripes) scores City's first goal.

But perhaps the greatest hero of them all was City's goalkeeper Bert Trautmann, who played the last 15 minutes with a broken neck.

A former German paratrooper, and prisoner-of-war, Trautmann overcame early prejudice to capture the hearts of fans all over Britain with his bravery and fantastic agility. He went on to make 508 League and 33 F.A. Cup appearances for the club—a record.

The man Trautmann replaced in goal was another football legend . . . the immortal Frank Swift. Swift played in the 1934 Cup Final, won 19 England caps and against Italy in 1938 became the first goalkeeper to captain his country.

Memories

Big "Swifty" retired in 1949, and turned to football journalism. He tragically lost his life, eight years later in the Munich air disaster.

Fans at Maine Road still remember Frank Swift, Bert Trautmann, Denis Law, who had a brief spell at City before going to Italy, and the rest. They also remember with bitterness 1963, when City started the season being beaten 8-1 by Wolves and finished it going down to the Second Division along with Leyton Orient.

Gates dropped and the shadow of Manchester United loomed even larger over Maine Road. While the giants of Old Trafford—under the guidance of Matt Busby, himself a former City star—grabbed the glory, Manchester City languished almost forgotten by all but around 15,000 faithful followers.

Les McDowell resigned, so did his successor George Poyser and his assistant Jimmy Meadows.

For almost three months, City searched the country for the "miracle man" who could work his magic and put new life into the sagging club.

In April 1965, City found their salvation . . . they appointed a new Manager. His name? Joe Mercer.

A few days later Mercer invited a brash, self-confident, often controversial Malcolm Allison, the former West Ham centre-half and Plymouth and Bath City Manager, to be his assistant.

The Mercer/Allison partnership proved to be just what City wanted. Together they formed a dynamic, powerful and above all successful combination.

They rebuilt a team with local talent such as Mick Doyle, Glyn Pardoe, Alan Oakes and Neil Young. From out of the Southern League came a 32 year-old full-back Tony Book, winger Mike Summerbee from Swindon for £35,000, George Heslop (a £25,000 buy from Everton) and Colin Bell a £45,000 untried youngster from Bury.

They rebuilt a team, insisted on a bright, bold attacking policy and within a few short months City had smashed their way back into the First Division.

Not Satisfied

Back came the crowds, but Joe Mercer and Malcolm Allison weren't satisfied. Something . . . someone was needed to transform this good team into a great one.

That someone cost City £60,000 from Bolton Wanderers. He was like Allison in some ways . . . brash, maybe too confident for one so young, and also controversial.

But above all he was a potential world-class star. He was, of course, Francis Lee.

The power of Lee, the scheming skills of Colin Bell, the elegance of Neil Young and Tony Coleman (a £12,000 buy from Doncaster) and the goalkeeping of Harry Dowd took Manchester City to their goal . . . the League Championship in 1967-68.

That triumph was only the beginning of a sensational run of achievements. Success that was to earn them the title . . . "The Cup Kings of England."

Historic "First"

In 1968-69 a Neil Young goal was enough to defeat Leicester City in the F.A. Cup Final. Skipper Tony Book, still going strong at 34, was voted joint Footballer of the Year, with Dave Mackay.

The following year City became the first English club to win a domestic honour and a top European trophy in the same season. Glyn Pardoe scored to give them victory over West Bromwich Albion after extra-time in the Football League Cup at Wembley.

A few weeks later, in rain-drenched Vienna, City defeated Gornik Zabrze of Poland to bring the European Cup-Winners' Cup back to Maine Road.

By that time new stars had been introduced to the Maine Road side . . . giant goalkeeper Joe Corrigan, defender Tommy Booth, and Tony Towers. And a couple of seasons later Colin Bell replaced Tony Book as skipper.

So Mercer and Allison had brought greatness to the club, now no longer Manchester's "second citizens" to United. But could they maintain their fantastic run of success?

Inevitably City slipped a little and again Mercer and Allison decided new blood was needed to put fresh life into the side.

Exciting Marsh

So in March, 1972, they paid £200,000 to Queen's Park Rangers for the exciting skills of Rodney Marsh.

Wyn Davies, who joined the club from Newcastle for around £50,000 in August, 1971, was later transferred to Manchester United to make room for Marsh and City fans settled down to cheer more success.

It didn't come immediately. Rodney Marsh settled into the side and won England fame, but there was unrest behind the scenes.

Then came the headlines. A sensation that was to rock the soccer world. MALCOLM ALLISON TAKES OVER AT CITY. JOE MERCER REPLACED AS TEAM-MANAGER and finally, JOE MERCER LEAVES MAINE ROAD.

The partnership had been broken. But Joe Mercer wasn't out of the game long. He became General-Manager of Coventry City and formed a new "team" with Gordon Milne.

PETER STEWART

While at City Joe had told SHOOT:

"Malcolm Allison and I are never satisfied. We're always wanting the team to play better. You can't stand still in this game; it's the way of the world in general these days."

Well, Malcolm Allison didn't stand still. He left Maine Road in a blaze of headlines to take over as Boss of Crystal Palace.

But City didn't mourn the loss of Allison for long. Just a month later they appointed Johnny Hart — who had spent 28 years at Maine Road — as their new Manager.

Manchester City's past triumphs are now written down in soccer history . . . and the club are surely destined for future glories. They will continue to find success even after Colin Bell, Francis Lee, Tommy Booth, Willie Donachie, Mike Summerbee, Mick Doyle . . . and all the other present day stars have been replaced with new ones!

Above: Colin Bell cost Manchester City £45,000 when they bought him from Bury in March 1966. He made his full England debut against Sweden at Wembley during the 1967-68 season . . . and Bury then received a further £2,500. Since then, Colin has established himself as one of the finest mid-field players in the world.
Right: One of the most exciting and brilliant strikers in the game . . . that's Rodney Marsh. He arrived at Maine Road from Queen's Park Rangers for £200,000 on March 9th, 1972, in a blaze of headlines. City fans soon appreciated his flamboyant and tremendously entertaining style. Rodney is a star who can on his day destroy a defence and score an "out of this world" goal!

TWO youngsters who leapt to fame last season were Sheffield United 'keeper Tom McAlister and West Ham midfield player Pat Holland. But in this leap for a high ball The Blade proves to be more effective than The Hammer!

WORLD CUP DANGER-MAN WIMMER!

WEST Germany and Brazil are the two favourites for the 1974 World Cup. The Germans crushed England at Wembley in 1972 thanks to a superb display by midfield ace Gunter Netzer.

Yet, according to Aberdeen, Netzer is not the man opponents should fear . . . it's his Borussia Munchengladbach team-mate Wimmer.

The Dons played Borussia in the U.E.F.A. Cup last season and most of their players are convinced that it's Wimmer, not Netzer, who makes the team tick.

The pair play together for club and country, so they've built up a strong understanding. Listen to Joe Harper, the former Aberdeen striker:

"For me, Wimmer is the better player, even though Netzer grabs the headlines. Without Wimmer I doubt whether Netzer would be as effective.

"Wimmer wins the ball well, and then lays it off for Netzer. But the feature that took my eye was Wimmer's running. Heavens, I've never seen anybody cover so much ground in 90 minutes. He's impossible to mark."

Joe's team-mates nodded in agreement, all impressed by Wimmer's unsung talents.

Davie Robb made a good point about the German forwards:

"Their shooting was unbelievable . . . so accurate. If they don't think they've got a chance, they won't blast in hope. They'll either work themselves into a better position or pass.

"It's disappointing to lose, but we've learned a lot from the Germans."

An honest admission. Perhaps the England players learned something, too . . . but few of them have admitted it!

POPULAR DOC

Arriving at a match recently, I saw a crowd of people standing in a circle talking. As a journalist, I couldn't resist going over to see what was happening.

It turned out to be Manchester United Manager Tommy Docherty chatting to a group of young fans, and they were thrilled that The Doc was taking the trouble to answer their questions.

Even though Tommy wasn't involved in that particular game, it was nice of him to take the time to chat to those youngsters.

The Midfield Star who turned his back on Rugby League

WE probably wouldn't have much trouble in picking a team of current soccer stars who played Rugby Union during their early days . . . but as far as I know only one has actually played in a Rugby League match. He's Liverpool and England midfield star Emlyn Hughes who turned out for Barrow against St. Helens.

WHAT have Norwich City and Crystal Palace got in common . . . apart from being League clubs of course?

Give up? Okay, then I'll tell you.

Well, they have both in their lifetimes been forced to apply for re-election to the Football League.

Norwich City had the embarrassment of applying four times in all in the old Third Division (South) and Palace three times.

Who, in those dismal days, would have forecast the tremendous progress these two clubs have made since?

When does a professional footballer reach his peak?

According to Ipswich midfield man Peter Morris it's between 27 and 30 years of age.

KEEPER'S CAREER SAVED...WHEN HE GOT THE NEEDLE!

Hereford goalkeeper David Icke took the needle . . . and his career was saved.

A youth starlet, Coventry City thought so much of David that they sent him to Stoke for a month so that he could train with and study the style of Gordon Banks.

Not long afterwards, he damaged a knee and arthritis set in. He was advised to quit the game. That's where the needle came in.

David had acupuncture treatment. It is a Chinese method which involves sticking pins in the patient's body.

The treatment worked . . . and David became soccer's first real PIN-up boy.

BEATEN...BY MILES

THE motoring organisations the AA and RAC were called in when little Berwick Rangers fell out with the Scottish F.A. over the distance between their ground and Dunfries.

It happened a couple of years ago when Berwick drew their Scottish F.A. Cup-tie against Queen of the South and were entitled to play the replay on a Saturday . . . if the distance between the two clubs was more than 100 miles.

If not, the match had to be played in midweek, with a consequent loss in gate-money.

Berwick measured the journey at 105 miles, but the Scottish F.A. said it was 98 miles. The RAC calculated the distance at 100 miles and the AA figured it was 97.

Berwick lost their fight. The replay went on in mid-week . . . only 652 fans turned up . . . and Rangers lost 1-0!

THE PLAYER WHO BOOKED HIMSELF!

Ballymena full-back Tom Gowdy is a name that referees can't get right! In fact, he still laughs over the time that Edinburgh ref Eddie Pringle booked him in a Texaco Cup-tie against Airdrie a couple of years ago.

Three times Mr. Pringle asked Tom his name . . . and he got it wrong every time. In the end, Tom asked the ref to hand over his little black book . . . and he wrote his own name in it.

Surely this must be the first time that a player has booked himself!

OPPONENTS PICK DARLINGTON'S STAR

Many newspapers give Man of the Match awards in their reports . . . but Darlington have gone one better.

Explains Manager Allan Jones.

"After each game I ask the opposing Manager to select the player on our side who impressed him most.

"It's not worth any extra money to the winner, they're paid to do a job and shouldn't need this sort of incentive.

"I introduced the award simply to add more competition to the game. Now if the winner has a poor game the following week, the other lads rib him something terrible."

MY MAN EUSEBIO

I'VE mentioned in SHOOTING AROUND before that Willie Henderson, the former Rangers and Scotland winger who's now with Sheffield Wednesday, is a great pal of Eusebio's.

Willie can't speak a word of Portuguese . . . and Eusebio knows no English—yet the two get on fine together.

On one occasion when Willie was in Lisbon with the Scotland squad, Eusebio was at the airport to meet the pint-sized forward.

Eusebio was driving an open-top car, and when Willie jumped in, he got into the back seat, clicked his fingers . . . and was driven off taxi-style.

When the Scotland team was leaving Portugal all the players were assembled at the airport . . . except Willie.

The Scotland Manager at the time, Bobby Brown, was anxiously looking at his watch . . . when Willie came running through the main entrance of the airport.

A yard behind came Eusebio—one of the world's greatest stars—struggling with Willie's suitcases!

BREEDING GROUND FOR MANAGERS

NO area in Britain can match the North-East for rearing League Club Managers. All these were born there: Brian Clough (Derby), Harry Catterick (Everton), Bobby Robson (Ipswich), Don Revie (Leeds), Bill Nicholson (Spurs), Bob Stokoe (Sunderland), Jimmy Adamson (Burnley), Ken Furphy (Blackburn), John Neal (Wrexham) and Lawrie McNenemy (Grimsby).

Within a space of eight months during 1961, Kevin Keelan played for four clubs . . . Aston Villa, Stockport County, Kidderminster and Wrexham. Now he is in his eleventh year as Norwich City's ace goalkeeper.

WHEN Bolton Wanderers met Walsall last season there were four players named Jones on the field . . . Paul and Garry of Bolton, and Stan and Chris of Walsall.

The same applies when either of those sides meet Bristol Rovers with Wayne and Bobby Jones.

Imagine being a TV or radio commentator at one of those matches with so many "Jones Boys" around.

It is now around eight seasons since substitutes were first allowed in the Football League and you may be surprised to know that many players still dislike that decision. The reason? No one player likes to be pulled off in front of thousands of spectators . . . and who can blame him?

MOST football stars prefer a nice, lean and tender steak on match days, but not Everton's midfield star Colin Harvey. He prefers cornflakes. "They give me lots of energy," says Colin.

The spell-binding 'WIZARD OF OS'

FEW players today are as exciting to watch as the multi-talented Chelsea striker Peter Osgood. On his day he can wreck any opposition in seconds.

His build, grace and skills are those of a natural superstar . . . a player destined to reach the top, whatever club he played for.

At times his seemingly lazy style can frustrate, almost anger the spectator. But a touch here, a flick there and suddenly there's another display of that Osgood magic.

And like George Best, Ossie has had his share of the headlines, too. His first-team debut, for instance, had the Press singing his praises.

The 'Wizard of Os', as he is often referred to, recalls his first senior appearance for the Stamford Bridge club.

"It was in a League Cup Fifth Round replay against Workington at The Bridge in December 1964. I'd been substitute for the first match at Workington but didn't come on.

"Anyway, after a 2-2 draw, there I was lining up with the lads for the first time. We won 2-0 and I scored both our goals.

"What a debut! I could hardly believe it afterwards. But I was soon assured it was no dream."

Two Medals

Chelsea went on to win the League Cup that season, beating Leicester 3-2 on aggregate—in those days the Final was still played on a two-legged basis—but the mercurial Osgood didn't appear in either game. Was he disappointed?

"No, not really because Tommy Docherty, our Manager at the time, had made one or two shrewd moves in the team which were paying off.

"They worked all right. We won the first-leg at Stamford Bridge 3-2 and drew 0-0 in the return-leg at Leicester. So that win at The Bridge brought us the League Cup."

It wasn't long however before the delicate artistry and goalscoring power of Chelsea's gentle giant had stamped him as a regular in The Blues first-team.

Osgood was on cloud seven and just when it seemed that his fabulous career had got under way fate struck a cruel blow.

Again it was in a League Cup match, this time against Blackpool at Bloomfield Road in October 1966.

Half an hour of the game had elapsed when the cultured Osgood and Blackpool's left-back Emlyn Hughes—later to find fame and fortune with Liverpool and England—went for a 50-50 ball in the centre circle. They accidentally collided and the Chelsea star was carried off with a fractured right leg. Fortunately it was a clean break of the tibia just above the ankle and no complications set in.

In fact, young Osgood made a remarkable recovery—Chelsea, in the meantime, had reached the F.A. Cup Final only to lose to Tottenham 2-1—and he became an ever-present in The Blues' side for the 1967-68 League campaign.

Peter the Great then went on to be deservedly capped by England in February 1970 and collect winner's medals in the F.A. Cup and the European Cup Winners' Cup with Chelsea, in 1970 and 1971 respectively.

Wants to Stay

But at the start of the 1971-72 campaign Ossie really captured the sporting headlines when it was announced by his Manager Dave Sexton that he was up for transfer for allegedly not trying in Chelsea's opening games . . . four matches without a single point to show for their efforts.

Despite all the speculation Osgood was eventually taken off the list and has since stated that he has never wanted to leave the Stamford Bridge club.

It's a safe bet that Chelsea are glad he remained with them, too.

Peter Osgood, the Stamford Bridge "sorcerer" (right), beats Leeds' Paul Madeley to the ball.

ON THE SPOT–

FIVE OF THE BEST

'Keeper
KEVIN KEELAN
(Norwich)

Defender
MICK MILLS
(Ipswich)

Striker
MICK JONES
(LEEDS)

Midfielder
TOMMY GIBB
(Newcastle)

Winger
PETER HOUSEMAN
(Chelsea)

What is the most difficult part of your job?

anaries 'keeper
evin Keelan
hows how
ifficult it is to
ut out a cross-
all, despite
assistance" from
is team-mate,
eoff Butler.

KEELAN——
Trying to cut out cross-balls, particularly now that wingers are very much part of the modern soccer scene again.

Having reached the bye-line, they swing the ball back so well that quite honestly, it could go anywhere.

A winger always spells danger and can be a nightmare for 'keepers.

MILLS——
As a full-back, I'm often by myself out on the flanks facing my winger. If he beats me he has the space in which to move . . . and the chances are he will have a free-run to goal. If, say, a midfield player is beaten, there is usually a defender to cover—but a full-back doesn't always enjoy this luxury.

GIBB——
It's difficult to pinpoint any particular part that is most troublesome. One week I can tackle like a demon, but misplace passes . . . and the next game my distribution may be spot-on. All games in the First Division are hard and different opponents have different strengths, so my own game varies accordingly.

HOUSEMAN——
Life for a winger has become much harder in recent years. Full-backs overlap so much these days—and they do it so well—that wingers have a lot of chasing back to do. Then, our roles are reversed . . . and I have to tackle my marker!

JONES——
I would say it's scoring goals. And it's agony when I go through a spell when I just can't find the net. But experience has taught me that I eventually come through it and find my true form again.

Which opponent has given you most problems?

KEELAN——
Newcastle's Malcolm Macdonald, without a doubt. He's a brave lad, has a lot of courage and knows exactly where the goal is.

Wyn Davies can be a handful, although I reckon he played his best soccer when he was with Manchester City.

MILLS——
When George Best was on song, there was nobody to touch him. But the player who seemed to turn it on against us was Tommy Jenkins, who was transferred from Southampton to Swindon last season. He had tremendous close control and usually gave me a hard time. He was dropped from the Southampton team on the morning of a game against us . . . I was well pleased!

GIBB——
I've yet to come across a player in the top Division who isn't difficult to face. The standard is tremendously high and I couldn't really single out any opponent.

HOUSEMAN——
I never enjoy playing against Leeds' Paul Madeley, so I was pleased to see his club giving him a run at centre-half last season. Personally, I rate him a great full-back, although he is so versatile that he is effective in almost ANY position.

JONES——
Tottenham's Mike England. He'll stick to an opponent like glue . . . well, I never get any joy out of him. He's good in the air, hardly gives me a chance to turn, in fact, gives me no room at all. I'm glad all centre-halves are not like him!

"Wyn Davies can be a handful," says Keelan, "but I reckon he played his best soccer when he was with Manchester City."

Which is the outstanding game you have played in from a personal viewpoint?

KEELAN——
Winning promotion when we beat Orient to clinch a place in Division One in 1971/72 will always stand out in my memory. But I don't think even that feat can equal our 2-1 defeat of Manchester United in a Fourth Round F.A. Cup tie at Old Trafford during the 1966-67 season. Norwich were rank outsiders at the time and United were going like a bomb in those days. No wonder almost the whole of East Anglia went mad at the time.

MILLS——
I'd select a series of games here . . . the 1967 Youth Tournament held in Turkey. We were beaten 1-0 in the Final by Russia, but we murdered them. I was very pleased with my form during the competition.

GIBB——
Three years ago we beat Spurs 2-1 at White Hart Lane in a League game. This was a wonderful performance by the team and I like to think I played my part.

HOUSEMAN——
I must mention Leeds again, here. We beat them 2-0 in a League Cup tie in 1969-70. Leeds were really going well at this time and our record against them hadn't been too good. All the lads played well that night and I look back on this game with happy memories.

JONES——
It was when I scored a hat-trick against Manchester United at Elland Road in the 1971-72 season. I didn't have a particularly good game but it always gives you great satisfaction to bag a trio against one of the top clubs. Leeds won 5-1, by the way.

Mick Jones recalls his League hat-trick in Leeds' 5-1 hammering of Manchester United at Elland Road in season 1971-72. Left to right, a Reds' trio of Alex Stepney, Tommy O'Neil and Steve James fail to stop Mick and one of his three.

Is there any aspect of your game that you concentrate on in training?

Ipswich defender Mick Mills, seen here during an England training session, concentrates a lot on being the first line of attack.

KEELAN——
I work hard at every aspect of my game. But, as I've already mentioned, cross-balls give me more difficulty than anything else so I do tend to concentrate a little bit more on them when training.

MILLS——
Although I'm a defender, I can also be the first line of attack. We practise movements from defence . . . the goalkeeper throws the ball to me, I play a quick one-two with one of our midfield men and then release the ball to one of our front-runners. This kind of quick attack is often very effective.

GIBB——
Tackling—but this isn't easy because I must be careful that I don't injure anyone accidentally. I'm basically a defensive midfield player, breaking up attacks . . . and starting them again in our favour. I work on the timing of my tackles in training even if I can't go flat-out.

HOUSEMAN——
Manager Dave Sexton works on all our respective jobs in training. For instance, I will pair up with a full-back and try to beat him. I put emphasis on taking corners and also do a bit of weight training.

JONES——
When I first joined Leeds I found that my heading ability was head and shoulders above anything else I did . . . no pun intended, by the way. Ever since those days I've worked hard at perfecting my footwork. You never stop learning about shooting and passing properly. I aim for perfection so if I get seventy-five per cent of the way there then I'll be happy.

Which player in your own position do you admire most?

KEELAN——
Stoke's Gordon Banks has always been my idol. But I also like the look of Liverpool's Ray Clemence. I rate him as an even better 'keeper than Leicester's Peter Shilton. To me, Ray seems to be the complete 'keeper.

MILLS——
When Paul Madeley and Terry Cooper played together as Leeds' full-backs, I thought their partnership was probably the best in the League. The full-back I used to enjoy watching was former Fulham and England star George Cohen . . . he was an entertaining defender. I couldn't select a similar individual now, though.

GIBB——
To be honest, I wouldn't say that there was one player I admire above all others. I have learnt that all First Division players have special qualities.

HOUSEMAN——
Three players . . . George Armstrong (Arsenal), Tommy Hutchison (Coventry) and Terry Conroy (Stoke). These wingmen can open up defences.

JONES——
West Germany's Gerd Muller. I don't go much on his work rate but can he score goals! And let's face it, that's what he is paid to do. I've got a great admiration for Newcastle's Malcolm Macdonald, too. He's always confident about scoring goals and he proves his point!

Peter Houseman is a great admirer of Stoke's Terry Conroy (above). "A player like him can really open up a defence," says the Chelsea striker.

Would you like to play in any other position?

Kevin Keelan and Mick Mills would like to try their hands at being strikers, like Spurs' Martin Chivers.

KEELAN——
I'd like to be a striker and grab some of the glamour for a change. I've a fairly useful left peg, although that doesn't stop the rest of the lads ribbing me that my right one is only for standing on.

MILLS——
I'd love to be a striker like Martin Chivers of Spurs. I know it's tough up front, but the rewards of scoring goals more than make up for the harsh treatment sometimes handed out. It must be great to receive the adulation of the fans after banging in a scorcher.

GIBB——
I tried playing as a striker for a spell but didn't like it. And I wouldn't fancy being a back-four defender. No, I'm happy as a midfield player.

HOUSEMAN——
I don't mind playing anywhere on the left-hand side of the field. Left-back, midfield or, as I do now, left-wing. I've had spells in all of these positions and enjoyed them all.

JONES——
I've never wanted to be anything else other than striker. I tried playing centre-half once or twice in a kick-about with the rest of the lads but I didn't enjoy it at all. I'll stick to scoring goals rather than preventing them.

SOCCER SHOCKS!

Derby upset the form-book when they went "nap" against Arsenal at the Baseball Ground last season. John McGovern (above, falling) crashes in the first. Alan Hinton (right, white shirt) scores number two.

ABOVE, LEFT: Tommy Docherty (right), a few days after being given the job as Manchester United's Manager. The Doc took over from Frank O'Farrell who was dismissed following one of the most sensational managerial upheavals in modern times. On the left is Paddy Crerand who became Docherty's assistant at the beginning of the year. **LEFT:** From television to touchline . . . that's Jimmy Hill. It happened during the Arsenal v. Liverpool League match at Highbury last term, when one of the original linesmen for the game had to retire. **RIGHT:** Oh the agony of it all! Sheffield United's Tom McAlister has just saved a penalty from Derby's Alan Hinton only to see the rebound headed in. Later, McAlister saved another penalty from Hinton, this time with success.

A hidden Roy McFarland (picture, left) heads in to make it three. The picture above shows the fourth goal netted by Kevin Hector (out of view). It's goal number five (right). Roger Davies is the scorer.

RIGHT: What a shock for England at Wembley in the 1971/72 Home Championships, when Northern Ireland stole away with a 1-0 victory, their first win against the English since 1957. Terry Neill (right) blasted home the all-important goal to prove that the luck of the Irish had at last come good.

LEFT: Leeds had to beat Wolves at Molineux in 1971/72 to win the Double. Billy Bremner (on ground) grabbed a goal for the F.A. Cup winners but Wolves won in the end, 2-1

LEIGHTON JAMES (Burnley)

BOBBY MURDOCH— SUPER CELT

WEST GERMAN idol Franz Beckenbauer was quite adamant about the ability of his Scottish midfield rival after his side had held on for a point in a 1-1 World Cup draw at Hampden several years ago . . .

"He is a player of top-class ability and his power is tremendous," said the Bayern Munich skipper. "If it hadn't been for him I am sure West Germany would have won instead of drawing. Of course, I had been told all about his skills before the match, but he still managed to surprise me and my team-mates."

The player on the receiving end of these huge compliments from one of the world's greatest and most respected midfield men was Celtic wing-half Bobby Murdoch, one of Scotland's most dedicated artists. Someone once said: "If Murdoch plays well you can be sure Celtic will also play well."

Bobby has been hit by an injury jinx over the past three years and since this Celtic have certainly felt the challenge of Hibs, Rangers and Aberdeen. They have missed the poise and the power he brought to the middle of the park . . . they have missed his astonishing ability to break through from seemingly impossible positions to score with his lethal right foot. It was that same right foot that pulled Scotland back from the brink of defeat against West Germany and so impressed Beckenbauer.

The Scots were trailing to a Gerd Muller goal when Bobby played a neat one-two with Charlie Cooke 25 yards out, swept past centre-half Willi Schulz and hit an unstoppable drive crashing into the roof of the net behind the helpless Sepp Maier to give them a point. Alas, the Scots still failed to reach the Finals yet again when they went down 3-2 to West Germany in Hamburg. Murdoch was injured and missed this tie and he was undoubtedly missed by the national team.

Murdoch joined Celtic, the team he had always supported, when he was a teenager and made the breakthrough as an inside-right. He quickly established himself in the first-team with a string of superb displays and soon won his way into the International recognition with appearances in the Under-23 and the Scottish League teams before getting his first full cap.

His Parkhead Manager at this point was Jimmy McGrory who predicted big things for Murdoch. His adaptability was breathtaking. He could play some games purely on the look-out for goals and the next could be setting them up. He finally settled down at right-half after Jock Stein took over as supremo from Hibs in 1965. Murdoch kept his wing-half position for the 1965 Scottish Cup Final against Dunfermline and was one of the main reasons behind the Parkhead club's 3-2 victory . . . their first trophy win for NINE years. How times have changed!

Murdoch went from strength to strength and along with Bertie Auld set up one of the most feared midfield combinations in Europe and, in fact, again starred in Celtic's greatest-ever victory—the European Cup win over Inter Milan in Lisbon in 1967. Murdoch made the winning goal for Stevie Chalmers when he first-timed a Tommy Gemmell pass from 25 yards.

Last season he missed part of the term again through injury, but Murdoch is now positive that his days on the sidelines are over. They have made him hungry for success. "I still have a long time to go", says Bobby. "I admit the nagging injuries got me down for a spell, but you have to take the good with the bad, haven't you? I would hate to think that I might have to leave this great game without realising one of my main ambitions . . . to win another European Cup medal."

RAY GRAYDON
(Aston Villa)

DEFENDERS OF THE EAST

Both Norwich and Ipswich did well last season . . . here are three defenders of the East Anglian clubs.

ABOVE
Full-back Clive Payne may not have attracted the headlines, but he played a big part in Norwich's efforts to avoid relegation from Division One last season.
RIGHT
Allan Hunter and Kevin Beattie (background) were as solid as rocks in the Ipswich defence last term.

STOKE CITY WIN THEIR FIRST MAJOR HONOUR...

after a dramatic and marathon battle against West Ham in the Semi-Finals and a thrilling Wembley duel with Chelsea.

AT Wembley on March 4th, 1972, Stoke City beat Chelsea 2-1 to win the Football League Cup . . . the club's first major honour in their 109 year history.

But Stoke's path of glory to Wembley was a tough one. After defeating Southport, Oxford United (after a replay), Manchester United (after a second replay) and Bristol Rovers, they faced West Ham in the first-leg of the Semi-Final at the Victoria Ground on December 18th, 1971.

West Ham were a goal down after 14 minutes when an unmarked PETER DOBING slipped the ball past 'keeper Bobby Ferguson.

GEOFF HURST equalised from the penalty-spot for West Ham, who finally went ahead when CLYDE BEST scored in the second-half.

Stoke fought hard in search of an equaliser but it didn't come . . . and the second-leg looked a formality for West Ham.

Semi-Final second-leg December 15th

If Bobby Ferguson had been one of West Ham's heroes in the first-leg, then Gordon Banks deserved the freedom of Stoke for keeping his club in the League Cup at Upton Park, when he saved a penalty from his England colleague Geoff Hurst minutes from the end.

Geoff hit the penalty right, but Gordon somehow managed to fingertip it away for a corner.

Before this dramatic incident, JOHN RITCHIE had scored for Stoke to level the aggregate scores at 2-2. And that's how it remained at the final whistle.

Semi-Final replay at Hillsborough (Sheffield) January 5th, 1972.

Both teams staggered exhausted off the pitch at Sheffield after extra-time with the score at 0-0, to drag their League Cup Semi-Final into a marathon duel.

So it was on to Old Trafford on January 26th for the fourth match in this League Cup saga.

Stoke clinched this replay 3-2, thanks to goals by MIKE BERNARD (now with Everton), PETER DOBING and TERRY CONROY. They just about deserved their victory, but the real drama came when Hammers' 'keeper Bobby Ferguson was knocked out saving at the feet of Terry Conroy.

West Ham skipper Bobby Moore refused to allow Ferguson to continue and finally took over the 'keeper's jersey.

Then came an even bigger moment of excitement on this stormy night of nail-biting tension. Referee Pat Partridge awarded Stoke a penalty and Bobby Moore shaped up to face MIKE BERNARD. Moore somehow managed to stop Bernard's first shot, but could do nothing to stop the strong-man of Stoke running in to drive home the rebound.

So despite goals from BILLY BONDS and TREVOR BROOKING for The Hammers, Stoke held on to their lead and earned a place at Wembley in the Final.

Above left: The Football League Cup.

Left: Stoke hug their 'keeper Gordon Banks following his fantastic save from Geoff Hurst's penalty at Upton Park.

Below: West Ham's stand-in 'keeper, skipper Bobby Moore, gets a hand to Mike Bernard's penalty in the Semi-Final replay at Old Trafford.

Left: Chelsea 'keeper Peter Bonetti is helpless as Terry Conroy scores Stoke City's first goal in the Final at Wembley.

League Cup Final . . . March 4th, 1972, at Wembley Stadium.

The teams:

STOKE CITY: Banks; Marsh; Pejic; Bernard; Smith; Bloor; Conroy; Greenhoff; Ritchie; Dobing; Eastham; Mahoney (substitute).

CHELSEA: Bonetti; Mulligan; Harris; Hollins; Dempsey; Webb; Cooke; Garland; Osgood; Hudson; Houseman; Baldwin (substitute).

Referee: Norman Burtenshaw (Great Yarmouth).

Attendance: 100,000.

Receipts: £132,000.

STOKE City walked out on to the pitch at Wembley to a deafening welcome from their ecstatic fans . . . supporters who were determined that the cold blustery wind which whistled around the terraces was not going to spoil the greatest day in the club's history.

Stoke didn't let their fantastic fans down. Showing no signs of Wembley nerves, they attacked Chelsea from the start and after only five minutes, a long throw-in by Peter Dobing was headed on by centre-half Denis Smith. Chelsea's defence panicked for a second and George Eastham flicked the ball back into a crowded goal-mouth. The flame-hair of TERRY CONROY appeared from nowhere and his header sailed into the net. Stoke were one up.

That goal shook a Chelsea side who were struggling to find their rhythm. But just before half-time the Londoners equalised.

Alan Bloor made a mistake in his own goal-area and PETER OSGOOD snapped on to the half-chance. Despite falling on the turf, the England striker somehow managed to connect with the ball and sent it past a helpless Gordon Banks.

Half-time: Stoke 1, Chelsea 1

Pacesetters

Stoke again set the pace in the second-half, but with the two defences tackling vigorously, play became a little scrappy.

City went ahead for the second time in the 73rd minute when veteran George Eastham—dramatically recalled from South Africa by Manager Tony Waddington earlier in the season—scored the most important goal in his . . . and the club's . . . career.

It was Terry Conroy who started the move. His pass found John Ritchie who pushed the ball into the path of Jimmy Greenhoff. Greenhoff's shot was parried by Peter Bonetti and the ball ran loose to EASTHAM who made no mistake from close-range.

Brilliant Save

Chelsea then hit back and it took a brilliant one-handed save from Gordon Banks to prevent Osgood from heading the equaliser.

This fight-back by The Blues seemed to spur Stoke on . . . and Ritchie almost made it 3-1 but his header was kicked off the Chelsea goal-line by Alan Hudson.

So came the final whistle which signalled victory for Stoke City . . . the club which had after 109 years stepped out of soccer's wilderness to the pinnacle of success.

The game is richer for their overdue triumph.

Top: Peter Osgood (on ground, right) puts the ball past Gordon Banks to level the score.
Above: George Eastham (partly hidden by near-post) slams home Stoke's second and winning goal.
Left: Manager Tony Waddington . . . the man who guided Stoke out of soccer's wilderness.

TONY & TERRY— non-stop schemers

TERRY HIBBITT may not have been able to claim a regular place at Leeds, but since he moved to Newcastle he has shown that if he had been given an extended run at Elland Road, the club might have decided to keep him. Terry played only 45 League games for Leeds, and one third of those as substitute. Newcastle gave him the chance to prove his ability and Terry's £30,000 transfer fee is now worth four times that amount.

WHEN Tony Green is fully fit, there are few better schemers in Britain. His soccer brain is always alert . . . moves ahead of other players. Unfortunately, Tony has been plagued by injuries in his career and this has undoubtedly reduced the number of Scottish caps he has won. Newcastle paid Blackpool well over £100,000 for Tony but he has been struggling to keep fit. Last season cartilage trouble kept him on the sidelines. However, Tony is still only in his mid-twenties, so he has plenty of time to catch up. He aims to make Newcastle the biggest name in English football . . . and help Scotland to establish itself in world soccer. Tony has the ability—let's hope he has the luck, too.

CRYSTAL PALACE PORTRAIT GALLERY

MEL BLYTH

JOHN CRAVEN

TONY TAYLOR

JOHN JACKSON

RIGHT . . . Tommy Lawton (dark shirt, leaping) cost Notts. County £20,000 from Chelsea in 1947.

ABOVE . . . The first four-figure transfer—Alf Common.
LEFT . . . Arsenal's David Jack, who cost £10,000 in 1928.

WHEN A 'COMMON' TRANSFER COST £1,000

Here are just a few of the most significant transfers between British clubs as a guide to how the record fee has risen—first slowly and steadily, and then really zoomed—over the years.

In 1905, the soccer world was shocked when Middlesbrough paid Sunderland £1,000 for the services of Alf Common.

It took a further seventeen years to reach £5,000 when Syd Puddefoot moved from West Ham to the Scottish club Falkirk in 1922. But only six years to double—David Jack was transferred from Bolton to Arsenal in 1928 for £10,000.

Nineteen years later, in 1947, Tommy Lawton left Chelsea to join Notts County for a fee of £20,000. Another thirteen years, 1960, and Denis Law joined Manchester City from Huddersfield for £50,000.

It took only seven years for Law's transfer fee to double! Leeds United paid £100,000 to Sheffield United for striker Mick Jones, in 1967.

One year later and Allan Clarke joined Leicester from Fulham for a fee of £150,000.

The £200,000 fee was paid in 1970. That was the total valuation of Martin Peters when he moved from West Ham to Spurs, Jimmy Greaves switching clubs in part exchange.

Leicester's David Nish became Britain's costliest player at the time when he was transferred to Derby County in 1972 for £225,000.

Denis Law (Man. Utd.)

Mick Jones (Leeds)

David Nish (Derby)

Striker turned 'keeper–

COLIN BOULTON

LOOKING at Derby County man for man it's not difficult to understand why, in the past two or three years, they have become one of England's top teams.

Colin Todd, Roy McFarland, Archie Gemmill, David Nish, Alan Hinton . . . all names that spell out immeasurable talent.

But Derby's march to the top might not have been possible if it hadn't have been for Colin Boulton.

He was very modest when interviewed:

" I always fancied becoming a goalkeeper, but I didn't think I was good enough. Every team I played for as a youngster seemed to be short of a striker and that's usually where I ended up.

"I joined a local side in Cheltenham and after a great deal of persuasion on my part I was finally given a chance to play in goal.

"I was 17 at the time but soon after my eighteenth birthday I went for a trial with Derby and as a result of which I was taken on as a pro. That was in 1964 and my whole soccer scene began to change rapidly.

"Reg Matthews was Derby's first-choice 'keeper at that time but he broke a leg and I suddenly found myself pitched in at the deep end. It was against Newcastle, who were a good bet for promotion from the Second Division at the time. Derby were in with a chance, too, so it was a vital game to both of us. But The Rams lost 3-0 and, quite honestly, I never stood a chance with any of the goals that beat me.

"For the next three or four seasons my chances were limited, even when our present Boss Brian Clough took over in 1967. During his first term with the club I played only a few League games, Mr. Clough having bought Les Green from Rochdale.

'We Were The Champs'

"Then in January 1971 I got my really big break. It came in an F.A. Cup Third Round tie against Fourth Division Chester, on their ground.

"We ended up getting a draw and, of course, we beat them in the replay back at the Baseball Ground.

"The following season, 1971-72, Derby won the Championship, but we had to wait a week to find out if the trophy was ours!

"We had met Liverpool on our park in our last match of the season. One goal won the match for us . . . a John McGovern scorcher.

"That was on the Monday before the F.A. Cup Final and Leeds, who were involved in the Final, and the side we had just beaten, Liverpool, still had a chance of clinching the title because they had a game apiece to play to wind up their programmes.

"Meantime, most of the Derby County staff, myself included, flew off to Spain for a well-earned rest.

"On the Monday after our vital last match against Liverpool we got word at our Spanish hotel that both Leeds and the 'Pool had failed in their bids to land the League and so Derby were the Champs!

"You can imagine the wild scenes. Even the Spaniards joined in our celebrations!

"Last season, of course, Derby embarked on their first mission into Europe. Did I feel nervous about facing the continental sides?

"No, because I knew whatever Derby's fate we could all look back on it as being a marvellous and worthwhile experience. And, of course, it was."

Derby County fans can also look forward to more unforgettable moments from one of England's most skilful and respected sides . . . backed up by Boulton, of course!

A near miss for Rangers' Alex MacDonald (blue shirt) as the ball flashes across the Stirling Albion goalmouth.

One of Partick Thistle's up-and-coming youngsters . . . Hugh Strachan.

Hearts' Alan Anderson (maroon strip) causes an anxious moment in the Dumbarton defence.

Aberdeen stopper Willie Young (left) and Hibs full-back Eric Schaedler are two of Scotland's top defenders.

Super Classy Outstanding Talented Scots

The new "golden" boy of Celtic . . . goal ace Kenny Dalglish.

YOU ARE THE REF

Study the picture-sequences, decide where you think the offence occurs in each one, then consult the answers below.

1A) When an attacker passes the ball towards the penalty-area you notice another attacker standing level with a defender. The nearest second defender is the goalkeeper. You decide to stop play and award a free-kick for offside.

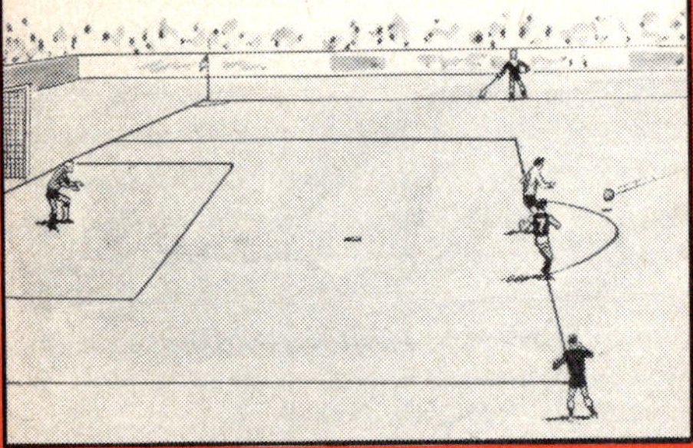

B) The defender quickly places the ball on the penalty-area line and plays it into the goalkeeper's hands before the attacker can retire ten yards from the ball.

C) The attacker turns and tries to distract the goalkeeper by jumping up and down in front of him. You stop the game, caution the attacker and restart with a free-kick to the defending team. Where is the problem?

2A) A defender holds the shirt of an attacker heading for goal with the ball, outside the penalty-area. Before you can blow your whistle the attacker is released and continues towards goal. You decide not to stop play.

B) The attacker shoots for goal. The goalkeeper saves the ball and kicks it upfield. You then notice two opponents fighting. You stop play, order them off and restart by dropping the ball.

C) From the restart the ball is kicked towards goal. You see a defender trip an attacker who is standing in an offside position. You stop play and award an indirect free-kick to the defending team. Where is the problem?

3A) An attacker is running towards goal with the ball when he trips over the leg of a defender who has fallen to the ground. This occurs in the penalty-area. The ball goes over the goal-line. You award a goal-kick.

B) Before the ball leaves the penalty-area an attacker runs into the area and is tripped by a defender. You stop play and award a penalty-kick.

C) The penalty is about to be taken when you notice that two attackers and one defender have encroached into the penalty-area as the ball passes over the cross-bar. You order the kick to be retaken after cautioning the encroaching players. Where is the problem?

1. The problem is in B. Although the ball is placed on the penalty-area line it is inside the area and may not be touched by a second player until it has left the area. The kick should be retaken. In A the decision is correct because the attacker did not have at least two defenders nearer their own goal-line when the ball was played. In C the action of the attacker is ungentlemanly conduct for which a caution must be given followed by a free-kick.

2. The problem is in C. The correct decision is a direct free-kick to the attacking team because you have not stopped play for offside when the tripping offence occurred. In A you have allowed play to continue although an offence has been committed because the attacker has a good chance to score. In B a drop-ball restart is correct unless you are certain which player started the fighting—in which case the award would be a direct free-kick against his team.

3. The problem is in B. A penalty-award is incorrect. The defender should be cautioned for tripping an opponent when the ball has not entered play. The game should be re-started with another goal-kick. In A the attacker has not been tripped intentionally, so there is no offence. In C the penalty-kick must be retaken.

ALEX CROPLEY-

The 'Englishman' who chose Scotland

Former Scotland Manager Tommy Docherty has a dynamic approach to the game—and he expects his players to have the same outlook.

One young all-action man The Doc wasted no time in picking for the Scotland team is Alex Cropley, the brilliant Hibs forward.

He thrust Alex into the national side against Portugal in 1971/72 when few people outside Scotland had heard of him.

There are two reasons for The Doc's swift selection. Firstly, Alex is a player of immense talent.

Yet, perhaps more important, The Doc knew he had to act quickly OTHERWISE ALEX COULD HAVE PLAYED FOR ENGLAND!

You see, Alex, despite a broad Scots accent, was born in Aldershot, Hants, but has a Scottish father.

So under the new F.I.F.A. rule, Alex could take his pick from England or Scotland . . . and Scotland was his choice.

He says: "Although I was born in England I grew up in Scotland and I feel Scottish. I was thrilled to be selected for the Portugal match . . . it was really unexpected."

Docherty, typically, gets annoyed at any suggestion that he chose Alex solely to keep Sir Alf Ramsey's hand off him.

"No player wears the Scottish jersey unless he is worthy of the honour," the Doc says with understandable pride.

Alex and The Doc had, in fact, met before. It was when Docherty was Manager of Chelsea and he brought 15-year-old Alex down to Stamford Bridge for a trial.

However, Alex quickly became homesick . . . imagine it, an Englishman homesick for Scotland!

"I have tremendous respect for Mr. Docherty," says Alex. "In many ways he is similar to my club boss, Eddie Turnbull.

"Both have an excellent knowledge of the game and can get the best out of their players."

Turnbull is reluctant to praise his young star too highly, probably because of the eager English Managers who would willingly write out a cheque for £150,000 . . . if Turnbull agreed to transfer his hottest property.

"Alex is a very skilful player," says Turnbull. "He loves to take players on, yet at the same time works unselfishly for his teammates.

Offer Refused

"I have seen many promising young players in my time and Alex figures with the best of them."

Turnbull has refused many offers for Alex . . . and there is an interesting story regarding one well-known English Manager.

Mr. X, as we'll call him, had been trailing a Hibs player for some weeks. After reading his scout's report, he decided to take a final look himself before making an offer.

Mr. X saw his player all right . . . but he also saw another one who was even better. No prizes for guessing it was Alex Cropley!

After the match, Mr. X made a firm bid for Alex, but Hibs turned it down.

A wise move. The Edinburgh club look to have a great chance of overthrowing Celtic as the nation's top team.

With Alex Cropley available, this task will be just a little bit easier.

DAYLIGHT ROBBERY AS KEITH TACKLES WILLIE

IN the League match at Filbert Street last season, Leicester City drew 2-2 with Manchester United. Willie Morgan was on the way to score a winner for United, but a well-timed tackle by Keith Weller robbed the Scottish international schemer.
RIGHT . . . Willie is on the ball as he spots an opening in the City defence.
BELOW . . . Keith sees the danger and rushes to tackle Willie.

LEFT . . . Willie realises that Keith is on hand and tries to rush down the wing to "lose" his opponent.
BELOW, LEFT . . . Willie seems to have succeeded as he runs for goal with the Leicester star in hot pursuit.
BELOW . . . Robbed! Keith times his tackle perfectly to clear the danger. This was just one of the thrilling incidents in a game that many considered to be the best seen at Filbert Street last year.

CYRIL KNOWLES (Tottenham)

Southampton 'keeper Eric Martin dives acrobatically to make a fantastic save against Manchester City at Maine Road in a league match.

TREVOR BROOKING...

TREVOR BROOKING sailed through his G.C.E. "O" and "A" level exams with no trouble at all. He passed in no less than fifteen subjects and his academic qualities have helped to establish him as a successful business partner in a plastics company. But when it came to learning the arts of becoming a First Division soccer star it was not an easy passage.

As a youngster, Trevor showed promise by turning in good performances for Ilford, London and Essex boys. He was rewarded when he was picked for the England Boys team in 1963-64 as a wing-half.

He joined West Ham straight from school and signed full professional terms in 1966. Trevor made his League debut against Burnley the following year —and his troubles began.

"One week I would play well," recalls Trevor, "and be sadly out of touch the following Saturday."

Then a real loss of form led to West Ham putting him on the transfer-list for £80,000 around Christmas, 1971.

"To be completely honest," says Trevor. "I was pleased when Manager Ron Greenwood decided to let me go, because I thought it would be in the best interests of both myself and the club if I left."

But nobody seemed to want Trevor. Then West Ham were hit by a string of injuries and he found himself back in the side. That is where his luck and approach to the game changed—for the good. In fact, Trevor improved so much that he was voted "Hammer of the Year" at the end of 1971/72 season by the club's supporters.

"I was very pleased to win this award," he recalls with pride. "Because it meant that the supporters had accepted me."

The midfield star nobody wanted!

SHOOT asked Trevor if West Ham's style of play had helped him to overcome his inconsistency.

"Oh yes," enthused Trevor. "Their attacking football has helped me tremendously and I rarely seem to have a bad game these days. They always think about scoring goals rather than defending for ninety minutes. Manager Ron Greenwood deserves a lot of praise for sticking to his principles and ideas about entertaining and skilful football because he has blended some fine attacking players at Upton Park."

Trevor really hit the headlines last season with sparkling and refreshing performances and a deadly partnership was born between the fast-rising midfield star and another favourite, Bryan "Pop" Robson.

Championship Chances

Says Trevor. "I have a high regard for 'Pop'. When he first arrived at Upton Park from Newcastle in February, 1971, he played in midfield and I got used to his style from being alongside him. And when Bryan moved up front it was easy to feed him with the chances to score—and he is certainly a great finisher!"

But what does Bryan Robson think of Trevor Brooking?

"Trevor was responsible for me finishing so high in the League scoring lists last term. I haven't seen a better midfield player in the First Division."

Things have certainly changed for the likeable local lad since being put on the transfer-list some two years ago. But what about the future for West Ham?

"If we can just get the results away from home," says Trevor, " then I am sure the League Championship is not beyond us."

And you don't need Trevor Brooking's brains to know he's one of the main reasons why the Championship can eventually wind up on West Ham's sideboard.

Despite being stretched to his limits England 'keeper Peter Shilton has his hands and eyes firmly on the ball.

The DOs and DON'Ts of GOAL-STOPPING

by Peter Shilton

IT'S a lonely life being a goal-keeper. He is the specialist. Every member of the team is equally important, but the 'keeper is the last line of defence—and, of course, he can use his hands.

This is probably the reason why 'keepers are asked more questions about their trade than their team-mates. Here, then, for any would-be stopmen are some of my personal Dos and Don'ts. I hope they help.

*Do try to catch the ball at the highest possible point, especially crosses.

By doing this the goalkeeper is making it more difficult for opposing forwards to make contact with their heads.

*Do dominate the penalty-box.

This is the goalkeeper's area, his territory. He must have command and he must make sure that everyone knows it—his own defenders and the opposition.

*Do shout.

The keeper must not be afraid to use his lung power to let his colleagues know what he is planning to do. A good loud shout will help to cut out mistakes and because he is behind the other defenders, the 'keeper has a better chance of weighing up the situation.

*Do keep your eyes on the ball at all times.

Things happen so quickly in professional football that it is vital to follow the ball. Concentrate on the game from start to finish and for goodness sake don't look somewhere else. Do that and you may find that is just the moment when someone pops in a snapshot.

*Do be brave.

Once you have decided to do something such as going down at an opponent's feet, do so—never hesitate. If you make up your mind to go—GO!

*Do kick for distance. A long ball down the middle can often cause a defence to panic and lead to a goal. It can be difficult for defences to turn and chase back after the ball.

*Do throw for accuracy.

A throw can lead to a break-through and at times can be just as beneficial as a kick.

Now the don'ts . . .

*Don't let the ball drop into your body.

My reason for saying this is

Peter says, "Don't stand rooted to the goal-line." Here, the England custodian cuts out a cross intended for Leeds' Peter Lorimer (right).

that it gives your opponents extra time. If, for example, he is 6ft-tall he may be able to nip in and get to the ball before you.

*Don't just try to stop the ball with your hands. Get your body behind it. Then if the ball slips through your hands, it will be stopped by your body.

*Don't stand on the goal-line all the time.

A good goalkeeper is always quick to come off his line to take corners and to narrow angles.

*Don't just be able to kick with one foot.

Make sure that you can kick with two. Two feet are better than one! Forwards will spot if you are one-footed and will stand on your good side to try to prevent you using that foot.

And now let me finish with a very vital tip. Listen to advice from the right people. I did and it helped me tremendously.

When I was about 14 and 15, Leicester coach George Dewis gave me some wonderful advice. Later on, I was fortunate enough to be understudy to Gordon Banks.

I learned a lot from watching him. He also went out of his way to teach me some tricks of the trade.

Call that luck, if you like. I had advice of the right kind. And it has helped me tremendously.

"When throwing a ball out (above), always throw for accuracy," states Peter. On the right, Shilton shows how to catch a ball at the highest point, to prevent strikers getting their heads to it.

BACK-ROOM BOYS LEAD THE FUN

"There's a guy in answer to your advert for a scout, Boss."

"Can't you pick the team on merit for a change?"

"He's the only one who's turned up for training."

"I can see what's up with our lot—they aren't fit!"

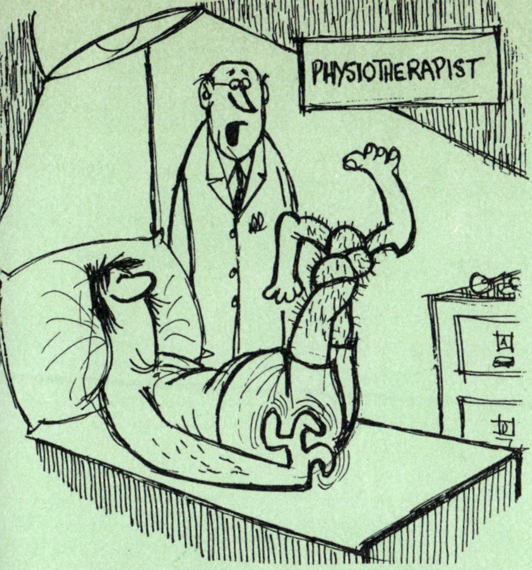

"That centre forward certainly tied you up with his dribbles."

"I've got the hic-cups."

"One of the conditions laid down by the cricket club on loaning us their ground—we keep the wicket covered."

"Same every home match—fling open the gates—rush back to the pay desk—and wait for the fans to come pouring in."

"Now listen, you lot—you're supposed to be going to the seaside for some serious preparation for a Cup match."

'FOOTBALL FAME, FORTUNE–

WHEN I was only four years old, I knew pretty well what Santa Claus was going to bring me for Christmas. High on the list of presents would be a new junior-size football, plus some tiny soccer shorts—and some little studded boots.

Nobody was forcing me to take an interest in the game—it all just came naturally. You see, I'd started walking by the time I was nine months, and my mum reckons I kicked my first football at that age.

Now I'm not trying to boast about my amazing physical, development . . . just stress that I found it pretty natural to kick a ball about even in the days before I knew it was called a B-A-L-L! My dad was very keen on football, so was my grand-dad, but nobody forced me. And if I had a son of my own, I wouldn't force him either, though I'd be very happy if he took a keen interest in the game.

Anyway — those Christmas presents were always something to do with football. When I finally learned to read (much earlier than the age of fifteen, by the way, no matter what the knockers say!), various relations would give me football books and annuals. Little did I, or they, know that one day I'd be actually writing in an annual like this.

Though I have noticed that there are a lot of people who knew me vaguely when I was a kid who NOW say they were always convinced that I'd end up in the professional soccer scene. Funny—because my own memory is of most people reckoning I was much too small to make the grade in the big-time!

But I knew in advance what Father Christmas was going to

By GEORGE BEST

BROUGHT ME AND PRESSURE'

bring. Later, as I started making a name for myself in the English First Division, I realised that the game of football itself was rather like a Father Christmas, always bringing me presents which I couldn't have got from any other walk of life.

Let me just paint a picture of the area where I was born and brought up. We lived on the Cregagh council estate, just a wee distance from Belfast. We were right in the middle of a working class area. Houses divided from each other by privet hedges, but otherwise each house looked like all the others. Even the front doors were painted the same colour.

Not much playground space, but there was always the road itself. Nobody even thought of playing any other game but football. Every kid on the estate, it seemed to me, was soccer crazy. More often than not, I'd be out there with the bigger boys, pleading for a kick at the ball (anything from a tennis ball to a tin can, or if somebody had a birthday, then a proper football!). Most of the other lads treated me gently enough, but I'm proud to say that it took a lot of kicking to make me cry.

Gratitude

Again, I had no idea that in years to come I'd have to take a considerable amount of stick, preferably without crying. And it took time to learn that retaliation was regarded as a worse offence than committing the original foul.

But the thing is this. As the streets all looked the same, and the houses, and the footballing kids with their ragged trousers and scruffy hair all looked the same . . . so there was a sameness about what lay ahead. Take my dad, Richard Best—just Dick to his mates. He worked on those big ships that were built, then sailed out of Belfast Lough.

And did he have to work! It's no easy job, labouring away in all kinds of weather, and with not much of a wage to show for it at the end of the week. While I was kicking a ball around in Burren Way on the estate, dad was slogging hard, wondering how to pay all the bills—and me, like most kids, wanting this and that all the time.

Football saved me from the monotony of the life that my dad had to lead. No false modesty from me over this—football didn't just come along and offer me fame and fortune. I had to work darned hard at it. Even after I'd mastered most of the skills, so that a football actually became part of my body, I had to work at getting myself bigger, tougher and more muscular. I devoted just about every spare moment to the game . . . and I was fired by the fact that excellent players like Derek Dougan, Jimmy Nicholson, Ronnie Briggs and Sammy McMillan had made the grade in England after starting in the same kind of junior football I played in.

But my gratitude at never having to sign on in that dockyard goes very deep indeed. But even so, my parents were sensible enough to know that I ought to think about some kind of career outside football. There was no guarantee that I would become good enough or big enough for professional sport, so the idea was to make me an apprentice in a Belfast newspaper office.

LEFT . . . George with the European Footballer of the Year award. ABOVE . . . In Majorca two years ago with film star Susan George. George likes this Mediterranean island.

In other words, I could have spent the rest of my life setting up headlines and stories about footballing heroes . . . and, no doubt, working myself into a right old state of frustration.

Football brought me relief from that, too. But I did have my taste of working in a humdrum office-type job. I was fixed up with a messenger boy's job in the Manchester Ship Canal company offices . . . pretty near Old Trafford, where I was an apprentice footballer.

That taught me, once and for all, that I'd have gone barmy if I had to stick at the job for long. I'd report in at nine in the morning, leave at 5.30 and then gobble down some tea before going on for training in the evening. Me—nipping round, taking lunch sandwich orders from the other workers, then telling the canteen staff just what was needed.

"Here, George lad—nip out and get me some cigarettes". It just about drove me mad. Four quid a week, day off Saturday.

No, you'll never know how pleased I was that football brought me out of that kind of atmosphere.

Even if I'd been made managing director at the age of sixteen, I wouldn't have liked it. What's more, it took all my energy, so that I could barely raise a gallop in training! And that really was a tragedy, believe you me.

Football has done a great deal for me. It would be pointless just to list the material things it did. Like taking you on a conducted tour of the Championship medals, the European Cup medal, the Footballer of the Year mementoes (both for England and for Europe).

You'd probably be more interested to see the scars, and believe me I've got plenty. Scars on my knee-caps, down the front of my shins, up there on top of my head even. Football brought me a lot of money, a lot of happiness, but it also brought me the odd moment of pain. You don't notice the way a bruise is coming up or a cut is getting sore . . . not during the game. But in the bath afterwards, and specially when you wake up the next morning—well, you know that you've been involved in a physical contact game.

I look back and I think that perhaps there's already been too much written about those things that football brought me. Every time I bought a new car, there would be a story and picture of it in the papers. I can see how talking about money in the bank, a new house, wardrobes loaded with clothes . . . I can see how it can upset other people. I probably would have been jealous of George Best if I had gone into the Belfast dockyard or a newspaper office.

But when I came into the game, there was a new personality cult thing going in the sport. Footballers became models, wrote stories, went on telly—there was hardly any telly when I was a kid, and there were certainly only a few sets on that housing estate where I kicked off.

Yet football has brought a lot of things which you can't sit down and just admire. You can see a painting, or a valuable antique. But you can't see what it's done for my personality . . . how it enabled a shy little chap from Belfast to become a pretty confident world-travelling bloke who can talk happily to Prime Ministers, top showbiz folk, and also know how to pass the time of day with . . . well, a dockie, or a compositor.

When I first started earning a few bob, I'd go into a restaurant and be scared stiff by the menu. So I'd stick to a safety-first diet of scampi, or steak, and always a prawn cocktail to open the innings. That way I wouldn't look daft in front of the more sophisticated folk sitting around me.

Now . . . well, if I don't know what a particular dish is, I call over the waiter and have him explain it to me. Waiters don't scare me nowadays . . . well, not much!

LEFT . . . Wearing a trendy suit, George leaves Manchester Airport for a tour of Bermuda.
RIGHT . . . George Best—This is Your Life! Eamonn "throws the book" at Georgie.
BELOW . . . Aged 23, George has a friendly chat with Harold Wilson—not about football OR politics!

Leaving aside a list of the things I actually own, I can say that football gave me a feeling of security. When I was fifteen, the idea of earning ten quid a week filled me full of ambition. I admit I used to go stupid when I got the odd big pay-packet in my hand—there were times when I'd spend thirty pounds a week on clothes. In the end, I realised that I was just being flash.

Contrary to popular opinion, I'm still pretty shy. There are times when I have to force myself to keep a conversation going, but when you're in the spotlight you learn to cope.

George is seen here at a wedding reception with Cathy McGowan, the television personality.

Friendships

Football brought me the chance to see the world, and realise that most of the world was a very nice place. It taught me that I wouldn't like to live behind the Iron Curtain, that I valued very much things like freedom to move around and do much as you liked.

Football brought me fame and adulation and also taught me that there is another side to the coin. You can be built up; and you can be knocked down. I used to envy the big-time fellows who were always being photographed and interviewed, and mobbed for a signed picture. And I learned that it's not easy to be sort of under scrutiny all the time.

I learned, too, that I was as likely as the next person to crack when the pressure was really on. That I could be quite bad-tempered if somebody got at me. And that sometimes you have to be cruel to be kind—otherwise you'd just buy yourself a whole load of trouble.

Despite the various ups and downs of my career, I like to think that football has brought me some lasting friendships—people who didn't blow hot and cold, but really tried to understand my problems. There's a terrific comradeship in this game because most people who play realise that it can be a very short life, that there's always the chance of sudden injury and an abrupt end to a career. I'm thinking of former team-mates, like Bobby Noble, his playing career cut short by a motor accident.

You get closer to some players than others. I've had what looked like VERY close battles with the likes of Ron Harris, of Chelsea, and from the terraces it probably looked as if we were not at all pleased with each other. Then we've exchanged a couple of jokes and a lager after the game!

Football also made me realise that you can get stale if you stick in one particular rut. Outside my working hours, I liked to mix with people from different worlds . . . fashion, television, advertising, even motor racing.

Football is a demanding taskmaster, and sometimes I admit I haven't been up to it, but it did the biggest possible favour for me. It lifted me out of an "ordinary" life, and gave me the chance to express myself in my own way in front of hundreds of thousands, millions indeed, of fans.

George Best

LEFT . . . A young fan takes a picture of his hero in Manchester.

BELOW . . . George is rarely far from a pretty girl—this time, Carolyn Moore was the lucky person.

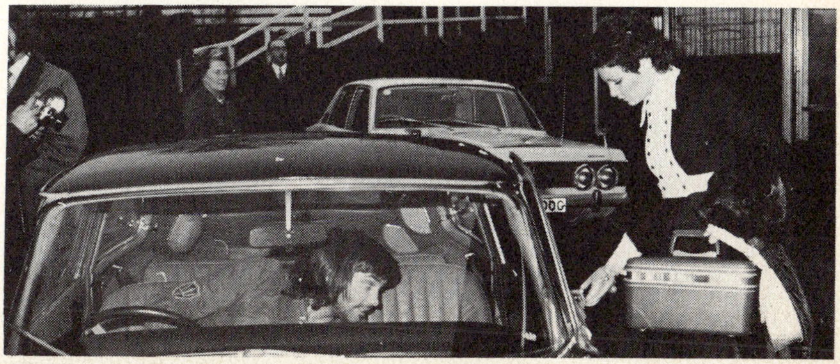

THEN AND NOW

THE name's the same but how they've changed! Here we spotlight five internationals whose long careers have earned them reputations as Britain's finest footballing ambassadors.

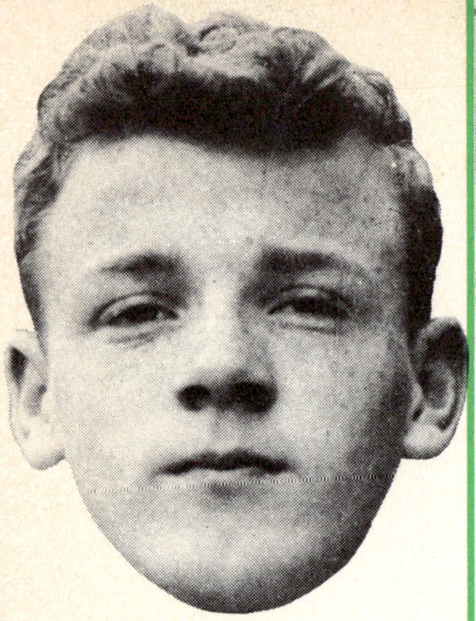

BILLY BREMNER

Skipper of Leeds and Scotland and one of the world's most competitive midfield-men.

Joined the Elland Road staff as a boy from a school in Stirling.

Earned a Second Division Championship medal with Leeds in 1963/64 and has won many honours with them since.

MIKE BAILEY

Skipper of Wolves and one of the best wing-halves in Britain.

Began his professional career with Charlton Athletic, eventually signing for the Molineux side in the mid-sixties for a fee around £40,000.

Won five England Under-23 caps, and two full England caps versus Wales and the U.S.A. while he was still with Charlton.

Completed his 350th appearance in League soccer in season 1971-72.

ALAN HINTON

Alan has one of the hardest shots in soccer and was originally one of the outstanding products of the Wolves nursery scheme. He signed professional for the Molineux side in October, 1959.

Alan later moved on to Nottingham Forest, making his first-team debut for the club in February, 1964.

Hinton eventually joined Derby for £30,000 in September, 1967.

He has won seven Under 23, and three full England caps.

JOHN GREIG

One of the most capped players in Scotland, John has made over 40 appearances for his country.

He started his career at Ibrox in 1960 and has since led The 'Gers to many major triumphs.

Although nearing the twilight of his career, John still has a lot to offer Rangers.

TREVOR HOCKEY

Born in Yorkshire, Trevor won his first international cap in season 1971/72—for WALES! His father was born in the land of the "red dragon." Now a midfield dynamo, Trevor started out as a winger. Before joining Norwich City in February 1973 for around £35,000, the bearded "driver" had seen service with Bradford City, Nottingham Forest, Newcastle United, Birmingham City and Sheffield United. Was a great driving force for The Blades in the latter part of the 1970/71 season when they won promotion to Division One.

Enjoy our light-hearted look at the

A…Z of football

A is for ACTION REPLAY, where you see your centre-half make the same terrible mistake again, only even more slowly.

B is for BODY CHECK . . ."but honestly, ref, HE ran into ME."

C is for CHAMPIONS and also CHUMPIONS. All clubs would love to be the former but, alas, the latter seems the more popular award.

D is for DOOG, alias Derek Dougan, one of the most entertaining and talented stars both on and off the field.

E is for EASY, EASY—when your team are three up with a few minutes to go.

F is for FOOTBALL SPECIAL or the Skinhead Express, where you will find more heavy boots than in an Army barracks.

G is for GOALS, which always bring smiles —and groans—to the terraces, depending which end the goals are scored.

H is for HOPELESS, a term often used after a player has one bad game.

I is for INCREDIBLE, a term often used after a player has one good game.

J is for JIM THE CHIN, otherwise known as Jimmy Hill. The "fun spots" on his Big Match Programme have had us all in stitches.

K is for KOP, Liverpool's famous set of supporters, on whom most other fans rely for their soccer songs.

L is for LAMP-POST, on which, it is rumoured, Liverpool iron-man Tommy Smith practises his slide-tackles.

M is for MULLER, the West German striker whose 1970 World Cup goal didn't raise a single smile in England.

N is for NETZER, his team-mate, who did the same two years later. Netzer's scheming ended England's European Nations Cup hopes, which again was no laughing matter.

O is for OFFSIDE, which your team never is.

P is for PENALTY, which your side should be awarded at least six times during every match.

Q is for QUEUE, which you may have to join before a game if your club is successful enough to attract one.

R is for REFEREE, who is always right and always wrong . . . depending which way he gives his decisions.

S is for SENT OFF, definitely nothing to smile about.

T is for TOP OF THE TABLE. Only six clubs in the English and Scottish Leagues can have this honour each week, which leaves 123 disappointed clubs.

U is for U.E.F.A. Cup, or Fairs Cup as it was previously called. English clubs have a great record in this competition . . . but we wish we were talking about the European Cup.

V is for VICTORY, of which every player is confident—until the match starts!

W is for WALL OF DEATH, which is how you could describe the line of defenders who stand in front of Leeds' Peter Lorimer when he's about to take a free-kick.

X is for SCORE DRAW, eight of which every pools fan dreams of seeing on his coupon.

Y is for YAWN, which you might do if the game is boring.

Z is for ZZZZZ, which you may do if you fall asleep when the game is REALLY boring.

CROSSWORD ANSWERS

from page 9

ACROSS

1. Invest 4. Educated 10. McNeill 11. Theddell 12. Tomorrow 14. Revie 16. Reside 19. Darns 23. Tonic 28. Phial 30. Bates 31. Marriage 34. Edition 35. Reissue 36. The Shots 37. Shanks.

DOWN

1. Immature 2. Venom 3. Stirred 5. Duty 6. Chelsea 7. The Town 8. Delete 9. Bloor 13. West Ham 15. Idea 17. Ian 18. Each 20. Ron 22. Sleepers 24. Outside 25. Ipswich 26. Norwich 27. Absent 29. Larry 32. Arson 33. Unit.

SCORE A SOCCER CENTURY

Tackle these ten questions and aim to hit the target of 100. Award yourself five points for each part of every question you get right. The Answers are at the bottom of the next page.

1. Study the picture above carefully. Now can you . . . (a) name the two clubs involved in this First Division match and (b) identify the player on the left? CRYSTAL PALACE EVERTON ROD BELFITT

2. These two players were transferred last season . . . (a) Johnny Vincent (from Middlesbrough) and (b) Brian Tiler (from Aston Villa). But do you remember the clubs they joined? CARDIFF CARLISLE

3. Is it true that . . . (a) Sheffield United star Tony Currie (far left) had spells with Q.P.R. and Chelsea before signing for Watford (he joined his present club in February 1968); and (b) midfield man Ralph Coates (left), started his professional career with Blackburn Rovers before joining Burnley (he signed for Spurs in May 1971)?

YES NO

4. Brockville Park is to Falkirk as . . . (a) Rugby Park is to Arbroath, Kilmarnock or Motherwell and (b) Cappielow Park is to Morton, East Fife or Berwick Rangers?

5. Can you name . . . (a) the Welsh club which sacked former England international Roy Bentley as their Manager last season; and (b) the Scottish international striker who was transferred from Rangers to Coventry City on October 5th, 1972?

6. Twente Enschede, Vitoria Setubal, Kaiserslautern, Ujpest Dozsa and Hajduk Split have all been in action against British clubs in European competitions in recent seasons. But which of these clubs come from . . . (a) Hungary and (b) Holland?

7. Mick Channon (Southampton—right), Larry Lloyd (Liverpool), Trevor Brooking (West Ham—below), Joe Corrigan (Manchester City) and John Marsh (Stoke City) all star in the First Division of course. But which of them is . . . (a) a full-back and (b) centre-half?

8. Can you spot these two famous clubs by the following clues . . . (a) Champions of Division Two in 1960-61, they won the League Championship the following season (they are now managed by a former West Brom and England star and are one of the leading lights of the East); and (b) League Champions in 1948-49 and 1949-50, their President is Field Marshal Viscount Montgomery of Alamein (but despite this army connection their traditions are naval)?

9. Kenny Garland, Bryan King (right), Erik Sorensen, Kevin Keelan (top right) and Tony Millington are all goalkeepers with English or Scottish League clubs. But which of them plays for . . . (a) Millwall and (b) Hearts?

10. Eddie Turnbull, Tony Waiters, Frank Blunstone, Bobby Howitt and Noel Cantwell are all Managers of English or Scottish League clubs. But which of them is boss of . . . (a) Plymouth Argyle and (b) Hibernian?

ANSWERS

1. (a) Crystal Palace and Everton, (b) Rod Belfitt (Everton). 2. (a) Cardiff City, (b) Carlisle United. 3. (a) Yes, (b) No (Ralph began his career with Burnley). 4. (a) Kilmarnock, (b) Morton. 5. (a) Swansea City, (b) Colin Stein.

6. (a) Ujpest Dozsa, (b) Twente Enschede. 7. (a) John Marsh, (b) Larry Lloyd. 8. (a) Ipswich Town, (b) Portsmouth. 9. (a) Bryan King, (b) Kenny Garland. 10. (a) Tony Waiters, (b) Eddie Turnbull.

95-100 points . . . Excellent. 80-90 . . . Very Good. 65-75 . . . Good Going. 50-60 . . . Average. Under 50 . . . Well, never mind, have a go at Score a Soccer Century in this week's SHOOT!

NOBBY
STAND A
HUGE CROWDS OUTSIDE THE GROUND TODAY
AND THIS LITTLE FELLER KEPT TRYING TO PUSH THROUGH
SO I TOLD HIM TO WATCH IT OR HE'D GET A THICK EAR
. . . GUESS WHO HE TURNED OUT TO BE ?

COLIN "SCORES" IN MIDFIELD

UNLESS you're a keen Everton fan you'll find it hard to believe that it's ten years since their midfield maestro, Colin Harvey, made his senior debut for the Goodison Park club.

But Harvey's baptism in the big-time is something he's not likely to forget in a hurry.

It was in September 1963 in a European Cup tie against Italy's famed Inter-Milan, in the magnificent San Siro stadium, Milan.

He was only 18, but despite the occasion, the noise, and the stories he'd heard about those hostile Italian fans the lad showed no signs of being nervous.

But even a highly promising display by Colin couldn't prevent Everton from losing 1-0.

It wasn't until six months later that Colin made his League debut—but after Milan, Manager Harry Catterick had no qualms about selecting him.

Although Colin has become one of the finest midfield men in the business, his early days with Everton weren't all plain-sailing.

Master Stroke

Recalls Colin: "I was playing inside-forward and was expected to score goals. Unfortunately, it didn't quite come off. The crowd began to barrack me and naturally it affected my game."

Then came a master stroke. Manager Catterick moved Colin back to the number six spot. Although the role was little different to his previous one, he wasn't expected to score goals.

Young Harvey's confidence came back, the Goodison fans began to applaud him instead of showering abuse, and he quickly became one of the game's most cultured and gifted schemers.

In the late Sixties Harvey became part of the now legendary Alan Ball/Howard Kendall/Harvey midfield trio. He was also a member of a side that played some of the most skilful and thrilling soccer seen in recent years.

But the game's top honours eluded Everton . . . until season 1969/70. That's when the men from Goodison added the necessary bite to their already undoubted skills.

By November of that season it was becoming obvious that Everton were going to take some stopping.

Then in mid-November came tragedy. One day Colin reported for training with an eye complaint that was beginning to make it difficult for him to see out of his right eye.

Specialists advised a complete break from football. Harvey was forbidden even to train.

He reflects: "It was heart-breaking. I couldn't do anything but wait. I watched the lads in action—and they were doing well, which made me even more determined to get back in the side."

And get back Colin did. In fact, he played a big part in the Championship run-in which finally saw Everton romp away with the title, leaving runners-up Leeds trailing by no less than nine points.

The following season saw Colin win his first-ever England cap when he turned out for Sir Alf's side in a European Nations Cup match against Malta in Malta.

But what has happened to Everton since storming to that famous League title in 1970?

"Yes, I know we had two lean seasons after that," recalls Colin. "There have also been quite a few changes in the side since then.

"But last season we started to reproduce some of that old vintage stuff. Give us a bit more time and we'll be back at the top again."

And who are we to doubt the words of one of today's master midfield tacticians?

AWAY WITH CHELSEA

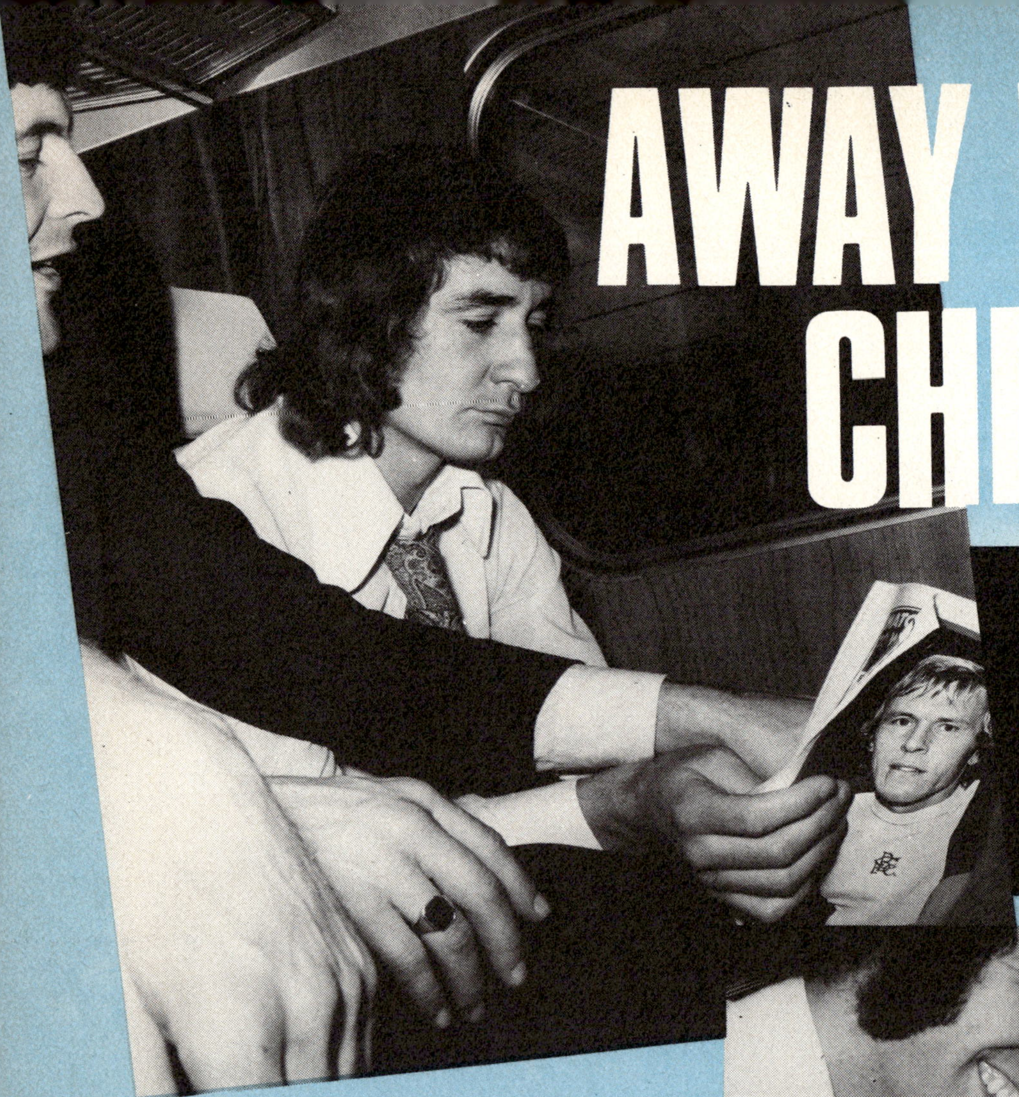

Join us with the Chelsea squad on a visit to Stoke and re-live the tension of the big match build-up.

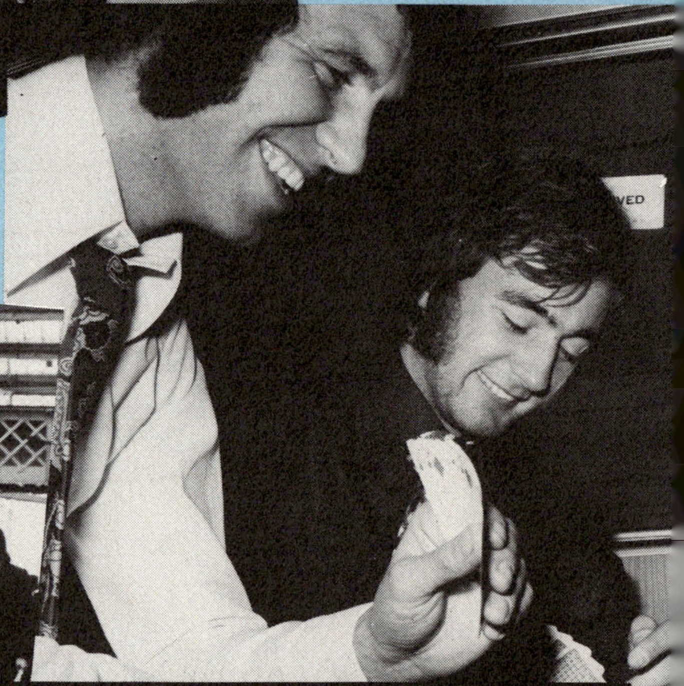

TOP . . . What better to do on a train journey? John Hollins and Steve Kember keep up to date by reading SHOOT!

ABOVE . . . Peter Osgood and Alan Hudson pass the time with a game of cards.

LEFT . . . The squad have arrived at Stoke-on-Trent Station and despite the miserable weather, they're in bright spirits.

ABOVE . . . The Chelsea players go to a nearby hotel for a light meal before the game. David Webb might be a tough-tackling defender, on the field, but here he assumes the role of "mum" by pouring the tea!

INSET . . . A few of the lads relax after their steaks by watching the lunch-time soccer previews on television. On this occasion, they saw highlights from Stoke's League Cup victory over them. John Hollins manages to smile . . . but the rest don't look too happy!

RIGHT . . . Half-past one—and time to leave for the ground. Goalkeeper John Phillips, centre-half Micky Droy and schemer Steve Kember walk towards the team coach.

ABOVE . . . The tension is getting more evident as the players are driven to the Victoria Ground. They talk about everything—but football.

TOP . . . The squad arrives at the ground on time and as he leaves the coach Ron Harris is cheered by Chelsea fans who have also made the journey north.

RIGHT . . . Manager Dave Sexton and club captain Eddie McCreadie test the Stoke pitch to decide what studs will be needed.

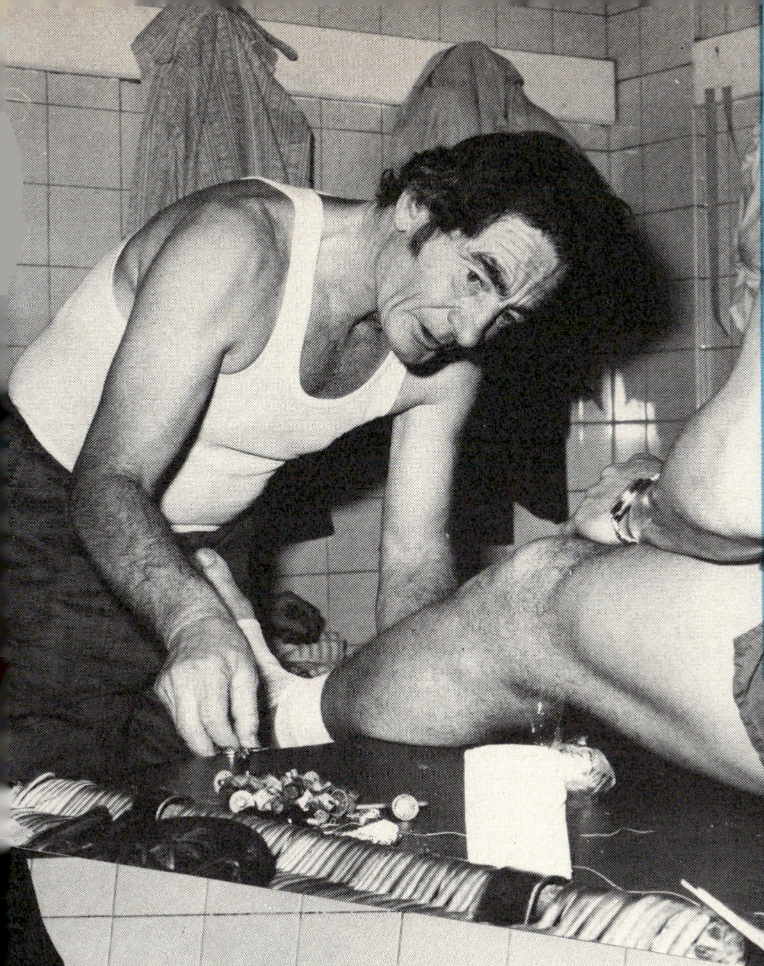

LEFT . . . Trainer Harry Medhurst straps a player's ankle just before the game. Harry also gives some of the team a massage to loosen their muscles.

BELOW, LEFT . . . The pitch is greasy and likely to cut-up, so Peter Houseman decides to change his studs. It's this sort of detail that makes The Blues one of England's top sides.

BELOW . . . This is it—the moment Chelsea (and Stoke, of course) have been working for during the week. All the tension has gone now as David Webb (right) prepares to tackle John Ritchie. The match ended 1-1 and Chelsea boss Dave Sexton was happy with his team's performance. At least it was an improvement on the 1972 League Cup Final!

NEWCASTLE'S "ROCK"

IF someone asked you what was the most established full-back partnership in the First Division the chances are you'd be stumped for an answer—unless you're a Newcastle supporter!

It's the St. James' Park pair, David Craig and Frank Clark.

Craig, in fact, is the longest-serving player on The Magpies' books, having joined the club as a junior as long ago as August 1960.

How did David break into League football, and what were those early days like with what is traditionally one of England's most famous clubs?

"It all began while playing for a Boys' Brigade side when I was working as a fitter in a Belfast factory. I had a short spell as a player at Scunthorpe straight from school, but I was very homesick and quit to go back home and start work.

"Then a Newcastle scout by the name of Matt Willis persuaded me to have a go with the club. I accepted because a friend of mine was on United's books at the time. Besides, they had a good reputation in Northern Ireland with seniors like the old fullback pair who were regulars in the Newcastle side before Frank Clark and myself—Dick Keith and Alf McMichael—both of whom played many times for my home country."

Craig, of the commanding tackle and ice-cool temperament, recalls his League debut for The Magpies.

"Unfortunately, I can't forget it. It was in November 1963. I was 19 at the time and Newcastle were in the Second Division. Stan Anderson, and Trevor Hockey, who plays for Norwich City now, were both in the side, too.

"The part I want to forget is that we were thrashed 4-0 by Cardiff City, and in front of our own fans. I was dropped for the next game."

But in the 1964/65 season Newcastle stormed to the Second Division Championship, with Craig playing a great part in helping them to lift the title.

It was also a season which saw Frank Clark become an established member of the St. James' Park outfit.

What is it like to have Frank as a partner at the heart of the Tynesiders' defence?

"Great! He's a marvellous player, so reliable. Both of us go about our jobs in different ways, though. Frank is tremendous at sticking his foot in and taking the ball from between an opponent's feet.

"I can't do this. I have to wait until my man starts to go past me. Then I tackle."

Which players do David consider to be the best he has faced?

"Well in my League career Imust go for Liverpool's Peter Thompson and George Best, of course. As an orthodox winger, Thompson, who's no longer an Anfield regular, gave me a great deal of trouble.

"Best, of course, was a handful for anyone. He must be the nearest thing to the complete player you can get."

The Northern Ireland international then recalled Newcastle's great triumph in 1969 when they won the old Fairs Cup 6-2 on aggregate against the Hungarian side Ujpest Dozsa.

"It was even more remarkable because it was our first time in European competition, and no one outside of Geordieland fancied our chances.

"You should have seen the crowds and felt the atmosphere after the team had returned from the second-leg in Hungary with the trophy. It's a moment I'll always treasure."

David Craig may have been helping to prop up the Newcastle defence for the past nine seasons but there are still several years left in the top grade for this redoubtable Irishman . . . years which should give him and his Newcastle teammates more memorable moments.

DEREK STRIKES FOR RANGERS

IT is never easy for a young player to hit instant stardom in his first season in the top team. It is even harder when he is expected to do the job in place of a big-name star.

But Derek Parlane, just turned 20, is an exception to the rule. The young Rangers striker came in for the Ibrox team last season after internationalist Colin Stein had been transferred to Coventry City for £140,000 and he immediately made the Rangers fans forget all about Stein's scoring exploits.

His ball control is first-class, his right foot shot is a fearsome sight and his timing in the air is almost perfect. But Derek has that special quality the fans love . . . he can put the ball in the net. He proved this in his first European game for Rangers. It was against West German giants Bayern Munich at Ibrox in the Semi-Final of the Cup-Winners' Cup.

Perfect Start

The first leg was a 1-1 draw and Rangers got off to a perfect start when Sandy Jardine put them ahead in the opening minute. However, the German side settled after this blow and started to hit back when Derek struck. He was in at right-half for injured skipper John Greig and moved up for a corner-kick on the left wing. Goalkeeper Sepp Maier punched the ball out and there was Derek meeting it powerfully with his right foot outside the penalty box to thunder in an unstoppable drive that gave Rangers a 3-1 aggregate win.

"I'll never forget that goal," says Derek. "It meant so much to the team and the fans and, of course, myself. I would have loved to have played in Barcelona in the Final against Moscow Dynamo, but I realised I was only in the team in place of John Greig for the Bayern match. I enjoyed that match and it gave me quite a bit of confidence.

Great Player

"Playing at right-half I often wondered if I would ever be able to hold down a permanent first team place because of the remarkable consistency of John Greig. He is a great player to have in your team and never gets half of the credit he deserves. When I moved up to the forward line as striker last term I was given all the help from my team-mates I could possibly ask for. They helped me settle in and the fans were superb also.

"It was because of the players' unselfish attitude that I was able to start hitting the goals I wanted for the team and myself. We got off to a bad start, but we proved ourselves before the end of the season. Tom Forsyth, Joe Mason and Quinton Young are all great team men and like everyone at Ibrox their main aim is to bring success on a large scale to Ibrox. And I am sure it won't be long before this happens."

Progress

Team-mate Alfie Conn says of Parlane: "His progress has been almost unbelievable. Playing beside him you tend to forget he is only a youngster. He accepts responsibility and, in fact, seems to thrive on it. Players of his age in other teams doing the same job may rely too much on their team-mates to set up the chances, but Derek doesn't.

Confidence

"He goes looking for the ball and has the confidence to shoot from any range and angle. I remember a shot he put in last season against Hearts. He was about 30 yards out and without taking a run at the ball he just lashed a tremendous shot at goal. The 'keeper was nowhere, but the ball crashed against the bar and rebounded clear.

"It was one of the hardest shots I have ever seen and would certainly have been one of the greatest goals ever scored at Ibrox if it had only been a shade lower. But I am confident we will be seeing a lot more of those sort of shots hitting the back of the net from Derek Parlane in the future."

AT HOME WITH DAVIE ROBB

Aberdeen

DAVIE has been a professional for almost 10 years and in that time has had a fair amount of success. "I'd dearly love a Championship medal," says the Dons' sturdy inside-forward. In the meantime, Davie displays (from left) a reserve Cup trophy, F.A. Cup Winner's medal, Drybrough Cup winner's medal and a Player of the Year award presented by the Aberdeen Supporters' Club.

When Davie isn't showing opponents a clean pair of heels, he's busy at home doing the washing-up!
Time to relax . . . with Davie's favourite singer Richard Harris. "I'm told I look very much like him," says Davie.

ABOVE, LEFT
Like most footballers, Davie is a poor gardener! Still, he tries his best—in between rests!
ABOVE
Davie would like to win a few more cups—but here he has to be content with a cat and a saucer!

ABOVE . . . Davie turns to a quiet game of draughts with his wife, Alison.
RIGHT . . . Davie with some opponents' shirts he has exchanged—he is holding one of his own Scottish jerseys.

'I'M HARD BUT FAIR'

says tough-tackling BRIAN O'NEIL of Southampton

It is probably true to say that no player has received as much criticism for being "dirty" as Brian O'Neil, the Southampton midfield star.

Since he arrived at The Dell in 1970 Brian's name has been linked with suspensions. His image is that of a hard player, to say the least, and fans at away grounds boo him at the least excuse.

From this image, you'd almost expect Brian to have fangs and a green tail . . . but, in fact, he's no monster.

"I don't take any notice of what reporters say," says Brian. "And if I'm booed by the fans it usually means I'm doing my job properly.

"I'm out there to WIN the ball in midfield. I can't do that without a certain amount of physical contact, but look at the size of me.

'Heavy mob'

"I stand 5ft 7ins and weigh around 11½ stone so when I tackle one of the 'heavy mob' they have an advantage over me straight away.

"Tackling and winning the ball is a skill and I like to think I can do this job well.

"I have never deliberately set out to injure an opponent and I can't think of anybody who has been put out of action as a result of me."

Fans may not see O'Neil as a competitive midfield player, but his fellow professionals do. He is admired in the game for his ball-winning qualities and the sort of spirit that wins matches.

Coventry General Manager Joe Mercer is one of football's best judges and he says: "Games can be won and lost in midfield and Brian has a great deal of influence in this department.

"He likes to be where the action is and this streak must give his teammates confidence. He's a tremendous player to have in your club."

Unfortunately, during the 1971 72 season Brian was OUT of the Southampton team for a total of nine weeks. He was injured for the early part,

and then under suspension later.

"I was getting booked for almost anything," he says angrily. "I was a marked man.

"People said I should quieten down, but in my mind I'd done nothing wrong and anyway it's not easy to change your style after so many years.

"All that's in the past, now. I never want to spend nine weeks like that again."

The real Brian O'Neil is far different from his popular image. He's quietly-spoken, rather shy . . . and back in his Burnley days even used to keep pigs!

Brian also has a quick sense of humour. One of his team-mates—who shall remain nameless—tells this story.

"I know I'm not the greatest of passers but Brian really rubs it in. He tells me after a bad game that our best player was in the stand, sitting in row H seat 36, because I keep thumping the ball there!"

You see, even hard men have soft centres!

IF Colin Stein had been a failure at Highfield Road, few people would have been surprised. Not that Colin lacks the skill to survive in the First Division . . . but Coventry City had, in the past, been a graveyard for centre-forwards.

Tony Hateley . . . Neil Martin . . . Chris Chilton . . . Bobby Graham . . . all had been bought to solve The Sky Blues' goalscoring problem. One way or another, they all failed.

So the pressure was on Colin when he arrived last season from Glasgow Rangers. Not only did he have to prove himself with his club . . . he also had to show that what he had done in Scotland, he could do in England.

English fans often say that Scottish players find it tough when they come south. Some do—but not Colin.

From his debut game against Crystal Palace—which City won 1-0—he displayed the sort of form that Team Manager Gordon Milne had been praying for.

Where others had failed, Colin succeeded. City suddenly found consistency and along with fellow Scot Tommy Hutchison (who arrived from Blackpool) Colin helped to make The Sky Blues into a feared force.

Ironically, one of Colin's best performances of last season didn't count. The game against Ipswich at Portman Road was abandoned with City leading 1-0 . . . the floodlights had failed.

"It's just as well they did," remembers Ipswich 'keeper David Best. "We won the 'replay' 2-0, but in that first game Colin was brilliant.

"I couldn't take my eyes off him. He ran into some tremendous positions and with luck could have had a hat-trick."

As it was, Colin scored only once . . . "I had no chance," admits David. "And I doubt whether any goalie would have done."

But how has Colin found life in the English First Division, probably the most competitive in the world?

'THE GAME IS FASTER IN ENGLAND'

says Colin Stein, who joined Coventry City from Glasgow Rangers

"The game is a lot faster in England," he says. "This is because there are so many players with a high degree of skill. In Scotland, few teams possess such individuals. Here, every team has one or two, at least.

"Deep down, most Scottish League players would like to try their luck in England. I enjoyed my years with Rangers and Hibs but I'm glad I joined Coventry.

"I'd heard a lot about the club before I signed. Their set-up is everything I'd imagined it to be—professional in every way.

"Nothing is too much trouble. The training ground, a few miles from the stadium is first-class and the treatment room is like a hospital!

"Gordon Milne and General Manager Joe Mercer have helped me a great deal . . . but everybody at the club has been tremendous."

Gordon Milne is, understandably, delighted with his signing.

"I bought Colin to score goals. We hadn't been doing this regularly until he came along but not only did he start banging them in . . . young Brian Alderson also benefited from Colin's arrival.

"This pair, helped by the wing play of Tommy Hutchison, made our forward line as effective as our defence."

Colin is a trier . . . and the Highfield Road fans love him. But he has a lot more than just energy.

He reads the game so well and his skill on the ball has surprised opposing defenders. Getting sent to Coventry looks like being a short-cut to success for Colin Stein!

KILMARNOCK'S
'MIGHTY MIDGET'

JIM COOK was shattered! It was his 21st birthday, a time of his life when he should be celebrating, but he had absolutely nothing to be happy about . . . his club, Hearts, had just given him a free transfer on one of the biggest days of his life.

But things have changed for Cook. He is now the midfield dynamo with Kilmarnock and is rated as one of the top middle of the park players north of the border. He was one of the main reasons behind Kilmarnock Manager Walter McCrae being able to sell Tommy McLean to Rangers three years ago. Kilmarnock needed the money, but McCrae said time after time he wouldn't let McLean go if he didn't have a ready-made replacement.

Cost Nothing

Then along came Cook. He showed he had class, skill and strength. He was just about the same size as McLean and proved he was capable of taking over his role. McLean was sold for £60,000 and Cook, who cost nothing, filled the gap with ease. The Rugby Park fans dubbed him "The Mighty Midget" after some particularly impressive displays.

He is a tiger in the tackle and never thinks twice about mixing it with opponents much bigger than he is. If you could compare his all-action style of play to anyone's it would be Leeds and Scotland skipper Billy Bremner. Jim likes to be where the action is at its fiercest . . . just like Bremner. He tackles and harries all the way . . . just like Bremner. And he is dedicated to the cause of the team . . . just like Bremner.

Jim is one of the most popular players at Kilmarnock, but sometimes his true worth to the team is forgotten. His unselfish running takes opponents across the park and leaves spaces for his team-mates. He is always looking that one move ahead . . . the one that opens the defence and leaves the road clear for the striker to carry the ball through before finishing the move. Eddie Morrison has scored countless goals from moves such as this with Cook the brains behind the operation.

Two years ago Cook was one of the main reasons behind Kilmarnock's march to the Semi-Finals of the Scottish Cup where they met mighty Celtic. The Rugby Park club were having a tough time of it in the League, but against Celtic at Hampden Cook inspired them to their best form of the season. He carried the ball over the park stretching the Parkhead defence and his team-mates.

Celtic opened the scoring through Dixie Deans just before the interval, but back came Cook to lead the Kilmarnock revival in the second-half. He raced through the Celtic rearguard and sent a neat low shot from 20 yards into the net behind 'keeper Evan Williams for a shock equaliser. It seemed Cook's courage was going to be repaid, but Celtic went on to the Final on a 3-1 score.

Cook might have thought there was no justice, but, like the professional he is, he got on with the game and became the power behind Kilmarnock's fight for survival. Life is full of ups and downs for Jim, but as he has proved in the past he has the ability to overcome bitter disappointments.

'I IDOLISED THE GREAT JIMMY GREAVES'

WHEN Sir Alf Ramsey made Tony Currie (right) captain of the England Under-23 side for the match against the Welsh Under-23 team at Ninian Park, Cardiff, in November of last year, it was yet another indication that the Sheffield United "hot-shot" could become a permanent fixture in the England Manager's future plans.

That wasn't bad going for a player who originally had played only around 20 first-team games for Third Division Watford before Sheffield United snapped him up for a paltry £27,500 in February 1968.

Young Currie joined the Bramall Lane club because while other big-name clubs hesitated in their respective assessments of the lean, blond striker, United Manager John Harris quietly stepped in to secure the rangy teenager.

Devastating

Other top clubs kick themselves today for not moving in then for the raw yet exciting stripling whose ability to score goals was devastating.

Currie, of course, has gone from strength to strength but life in his early days with The Blades was frustrating and near-heartbreaking.

Less than three months after joining the Sheffield club, Currie and company found themselves relegated to the Second Division.

But in the 1970-71 season they bounced back again and have since become one of the most exciting sides to watch in soccer's top sphere.

There's been a change of playing style for The Blades' blond star, too. He now displays his tremendous talents more in midfield, waiting for the chance to race through and terrorise rearguards with his goal-grabbing prowess.

When Tony was asked whether he missed being an out-and-out striker, he replied:

"No—because on reflection, I realise that in my early days at Bramall Lane I never really made a great impression as a goal-scorer, despite the reputation I'd got at Watford. It wasn't until Mr. Harris moved me to a midfield position that things started to buzz for me.

"I have no regrets at all about switching from a striking role. The move to midfield has been the best thing that has ever happened to me. I'm always involved in the game, and this suits me admirably. It still allows me to come forward, though, and have a go at goal."

Currie then talked at length about how his career has progressed since signing for The Blades.

"Let me tell you straight away that my progress wouldn't have been possible if it hadn't been for the tremendous help I've had from the rest of the lads here. Sheffield United are certainly a great club to belong to.

"Out on the park we've never been content to sacrifice all the flair present in the side, even when things haven't been going well for us."

"The coaching staff at Bramall Lane must be among the best in the First Division, and I've got a great deal to thank them for.

"And I'll tell you this, no youngster wanting to make an impression on the game could wish for a better Manager than Mr. Harris. He doesn't say very much, but don't be misled by his apparently reserved attitude. The boss knows all there is to know about the game, believe me."

Fantastic

Tony was then asked if he had any soccer idols when he was a boy?

'Yes, Jimmy Greaves. I used to go and watch Chelsea regularly as a lad and never took my eyes off him.

"To be honest, I idolised him. His goalscoring feats were fantastic. I'll be satisfied if I'm only half the success Jim was as a player."

The odds are that Tony Currie at 23 will become just as successful as the little genius he used to worship from the terraces at Stamford Bridge.

The tall, blond midfield star is not unlike West Germany's Gunter Netzer as he surges forward towards goal, with his long hair flowing out behind him and power and menace in his every stride.

England Manager Sir Alf Ramsey was once quoted as saying that Netzer was possibly the most exciting player in Europe.

Tony cannot rank far behind!

Behind the scenes at Ipswich

PERHAPS it is a little unkind to call Ipswich Town the "surprise" team of last season . . . but nevertheless, the East Anglian club shook the soccer world with their brilliant performances, especially away from home. What-and-who makes the Town tick? The **SHOOT** photographer went behind the scenes at Portman Road to find out.

TOP . . . It's defence versus attack as Ipswich practise in their gymnasium.

ABOVE . . . Track-suited Manager Bobby Robson is obviously in charge of this training session.

LEFT . . . The cantilever stand at Portman Road, which was opened by former Manager Sir Alf Ramsey in 1971.

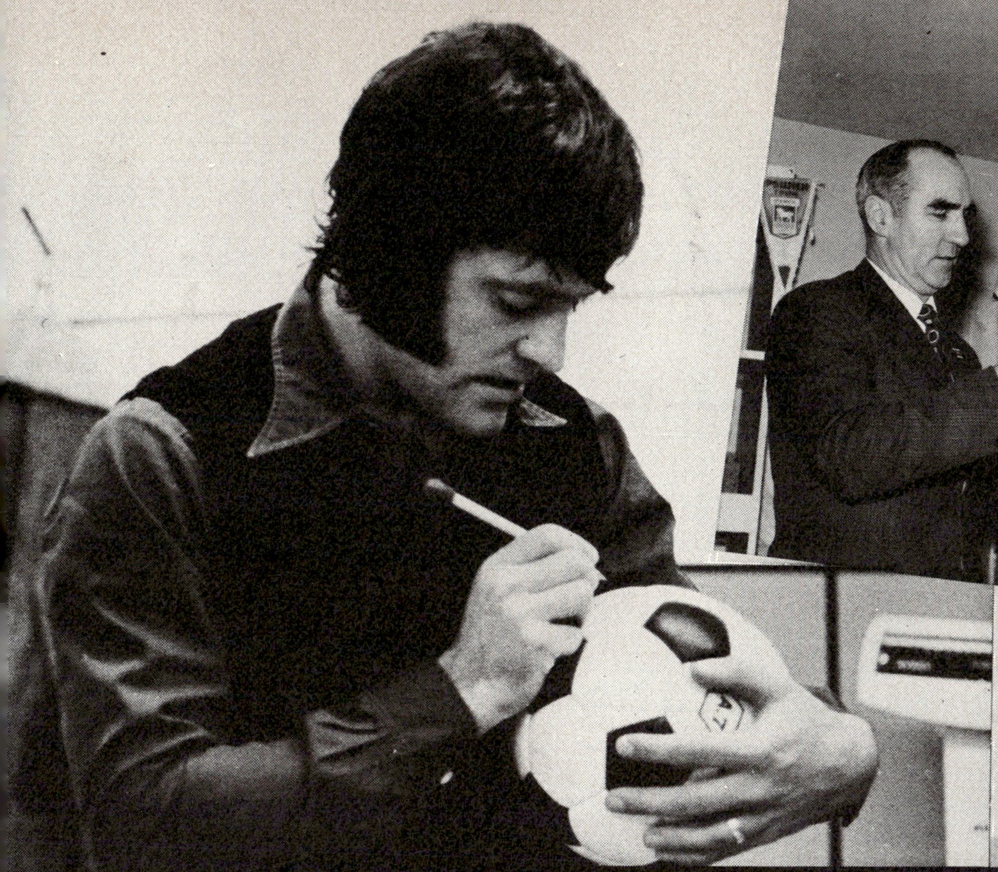

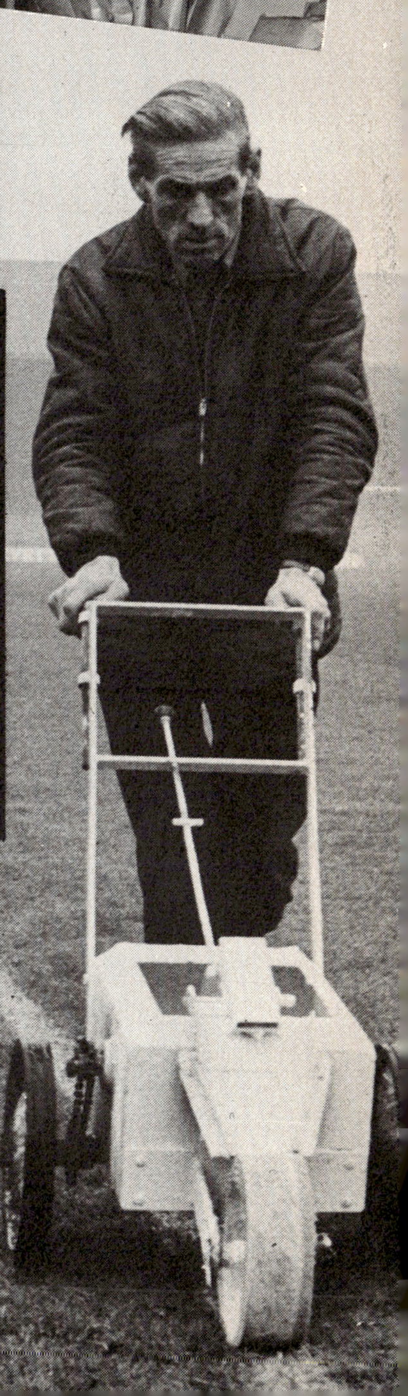

ABOVE, LEFT . . Midfield man Peter Morris autographs a ball for a fan.

TOP RIGHT . . . Tom Parker, the club's Promoter, checks to ensure that the goods in the souvenir shop are in tip-top shape.

RIGHT . . . Head Groundsman Stan Prendergast can boast possibly the best pitch in the League. Here, we see him marking the six-yard box.

BELOW . . . A top star can never escape the anxious autograph hunters—not that he wants to! Striker David Johnson helps out on this occasion.

TOP, LEFT . . . Walter Gray, the Honorary Secretary, answers the phone that somehow never stops ringing. That's the price of fame—and Ipswich like it.

TOP . . . The man who has made Ipswich one of the most feared sides in the League—Manager Bobby Robson.

ABOVE . . . Assistant Promoter Basil Acres helps out a fan with a query about a souvenir.

LEFT . . . Receptionists Una Dedman (sitting) and Pat Godbold add glamour to a club now striving to establish a successful First Division tradition!

DENIS McQUADE (Partick Thistle)

LEIGHTON PHILLIPS
Cardiff and Wales

DEREK DOUGAN
Wolves and N. Ireland

BRITISH AND BEST

COLIN BELL
Manchester City and England

GEORGE GRAHAM
Manchester United and Scotland

MARTIN DOBSON
(Burnley)

KENNY GARLAND–'keeper courageous

"KENNY Garland for Scotland" . . . that is the cry that rings round Tynecastle as the big Hearts 'keeper makes one breath-taking save after another. It is an amazing about-turn in soccer fortunes for 'keeper Kenny.

For seven years he played with consistency in the Hearts reserves, but he just couldn't dislodge Jim Cruickshank from the first-team. Cruickshank was a great favourite with the Edinburgh fans and was rated as one of the best 'keepers in the business. He was capped by Scotland and he looked like going on forever.

But Garland took it all in his stride with quiet confidence. He realised he had the ability to hold down a top team place with a First Division club and he was prepared to wait for the break-through. He asked for a transfer three years ago and was put on the list, but Hearts didn't receive one single concrete offer for his services.

Undeterred, Kenny played away in the second-team when suddenly two years ago and quite unexpectedly he was launched into the first-team in place of Cruickshank.

Manager Bobby Seith, the former Preston boss, has given Kenny his chance to settle in and he has certainly taken it as positively with both hands as he would a cross-ball. Watching Garland perform, it is difficult to envisage him stuck in the reserves for such a long time. Last season he was one of the most consistent 'keepers in Scotland and reserved some of his top performances for the really big games.

When Hearts beat Rangers 1-0 at Ibrox, Kenny had the home players shaking their heads in disbelief time after time with his anticipation, agility and courage. He is definitely one of the bravest 'keepers in the game.

Happy With Hearts

Now that Kenny has broken through with Hearts, is there any chance of him going all the way and getting into the Scotland team? "That would be nice," says Kenny, "but at the moment I am happy to consolidate my place with Hearts. I never really wanted to leave Tynecastle when I asked for a transfer, but I felt I had to if I was ever to do something in the game.

"I am as ambitious as the next bloke and, let's face it, Jim Cruickshank's form over the years was simply incredible. I wanted first-team soccer and now that I have it without leaving Hearts I am delighted. They are a great club with great support and things are beginning to buzz again in Edinburgh. I want to be in on that."

Kenny's catalogue of super saves is vast and it would be difficult for him to select his best one. However, the fans who saw him last season in the League match against Airdrie at Broomfield are adamant that he won't better the save he had in that game.

Tremendous Save

Hearts were leading 2-0 with only four minutes left to go and Kenny may have been forgiven if he let his concentration slip for a second. But he didn't and was able to pull off the sort of save that has EVERY fan in the ground cheering. His magnificent effort came after Derek Whiteford had slipped a short free-kick to Tommy Walker. The Airdrie player summoned all the power in his frame into one vital moment of impact and met the ball first-time to lash a ferocious shot towards the left hand corner of the net. The Airdrie fans were already claiming a goal when Garland somersaulted across his line to push the ball round the post at full-stretch in tremendous acrobatic fashion!

A great 'keeper with a fine future ahead of him!

DON GOES FOR HIS SECOND 'TON'

WITH Swindon Town, Don Rogers always looked a great player. At Wembley in 1969, millions of television viewers saw him destroy mighty Arsenal in The Robins' League Cup victory.

But before a player can truthfully be called great he has to prove himself amongst the giants of Division One . . . and dashing Don hadn't done that.

Until November 4th, 1972 that is. This was the date of Don's long overdue debut in the First Division . . . for Crystal Palace, against Everton.

To say Don was an immediate success is almost understating the effect he had on Palace.

When he joined the club, they were bottom of Division One with nine points from a possible 30.

In the next four League games Palace were unbeaten, collecting five points.

Of course, no one man makes a team, yet Don obviously had the sort of effect on the side General Manager Bert Head dreamed of.

In his debut, Don scored a magnificent solo goal, sliding the ball home with the precision of a surgeon.

His second game saw his second goal . . . against Derby at the Baseball Ground.

Charlie Cooke, who signed for Palace shortly before Don, says: "He is a brilliant player, make no mistake about it. Don loves to attack defences on his own and this sort of confidence quickly spread through the team.

"He holds the ball so well, waiting until a team-mate runs into position before passing."

But how does Don himself sum up his first year in the big time?

"Two things surprised me about Division One football," he says. "Firstly, the pace is shattering compared with the Second Division.

"And from watching games on television, I had the impression that most teams were defensive.

"I was wrong. With Swindon, I often had to come deep to gain possession and then run at the opposition.

"With Palace, I stay up front most of the time and opponents have often been caught out because their defenders are in our half of the pitch."

Wanted a 'Move'

Don spent 10 years at Swindon and appeared in almost 400 League games, scoring around 150 goals . . . a good average for a winger . . . and he's hoping to get the goal that will notch up his second "ton" at Selhurst Park.

Many people feel that if Don had moved earlier, he would have won international honours, even though England Manager Sir Alf Ramsey prefers not to use wingmen.

Had Don any regrets about his stay with Swindon?

"I had wanted a move for years, but the chance just didn't come. The club were reluctant to sell me and I only found out about any inquiry for me when it was too late.

"When Crystal Palace made a firm offer and the Swindon Board decided I could go, I was thrilled.

"I worked under Bert Head when he was with Swindon and I've always admired him. Perhaps I was a late starter at 27, but this made me even more keen to show everybody what I could do.

"My aim has always been to get to the top. Now, with Palace, I'd like to think we can get there."

Don is the type of player all supporters love to watch. His speed can leave any defence stranded . . . his close-control can fool even the tightest of markers . . . and his explosive shooting makes him a natural for television's goal competitions.

It is a shame that Don had to wait so long to prove that he can turn it on in Division One.

But Palace fans will tell you that it's definitely better late than never!

SECOND DIVISION– BUT FIRST RATE

SWINDON'S goal in the past few seasons has been First Division soccer. They haven't made it, but a regular service of goals from Eire international Ray Treacy (below) will help The Railwaymen to keep on the right track.

THE ball is safely in the arms of Sheffield Wednesday 'keeper Peter Grummitt (above). And it's a safe bet the expert handling of Peter will bring the famous Hillsborough club more honours.

HENRY NEWTON (Everton)

RANGERS' NIGHT

wrecked by the 'Battle of Barcelona'

European Cup-Winners' Cup Final (May 24th, 1972)
RANGERS (2) 3 v. MOSCOW DYNAMO (0) 2

THE TEAMS

RANGERS: McCloy; Jardine; Mathieson; Greig; Johnstone; D. Smith; McLean; Conn; Stein; Macdonald; Johnston, W.
MOSCOW DYNAMO: Pilgui; Basalev; Dolmatov; Zykov; Dobbonosov (sub. Gerschkovitch); Zhukov; Baidatchni; Jakvbik (sub. Eshtrekov); Sabo; Mahovikov; Evryuzhikin.
Referee: Jose Ortiz di Mendibil (Spain)

Colin Stein (extreme left) beats Moscow Dynamo 'keeper Pilgui to score Rangers' first goal in Barcelona.

BRILLIANT Rangers deservedly defeated Moscow Dynamo in the Camp Nou Stadium, Barcelona, to win the European Cup-Winners' Cup. Eleven blue-shirted heroes fought magnificently to capture the club's first major honour in Europe.

But this historic occasion was paradoxically a night to remember . . . and one to forget . . . because Rangers' triumph was virtually wiped out by the disgraceful behaviour of a section of their fans who ran riot at the end.

Around 25,000 Rangers supporters had travelled from Glasgow and they saw their heroes take control of the game from the start . . . which had been delayed by fans who invaded the pitch as the teams were led out.

Rangers attacked the Russians in a non-stop wave of blue-shirts and inevitably went ahead in the 24th minute when COLIN STEIN (now with Coventry) took a pass from Dave Smith in his stride and smashed a thunderous shot past 'keeper Pilgui.

Once in the lead, Rangers seemed unstoppable and five minutes before half-time scored a second.

Once again magnificent Dave Smith was the architect of the goal. His inch-perfect free-kick found WILLIE JOHNSTON (now at West Brom) who headed past Pilgui.

When Rangers went 3-0 up shortly after the restart—thanks to another brilliant goal by WILLIE JOHNSTON—they had every right to sense victory. But Dynamo were far from being beaten.

On the hour they struck back when ESHTREKOV, who had come on as a substitute a couple of minutes earlier, punished a mistake by the Rangers defence with a well-taken goal.

The Russians were now very much back in the game and at times Rangers were forced to defend desperately. Then four minutes from the end, Dynamo cut Rangers lead to 3-2 when MAHOVIKOV scored.

Despite a furious onslaught by the Russians, Rangers held on until the final whistle.

But then came the invasion of fans. Players and officials were swamped by the delirious mob. So wild were the scenes, as Spanish riot police moved in, that the Cup had to be presented to skipper John Greig in the safety of the dressing-room.

But the rioting on the field and in the city of Barcelona went on.

Finally the police gained control. The many thousands of true, decent fans returned to Glasgow . . . along with the hooligan minority.

But the damage had been done. The Final of the 1972 European Cup-Winners' Cup—a magnificent moment of glory for Rangers—will not be remembered for the football that was played but for the notorious, violent scenes that followed. Sadly for this great and famous club that Final will always be called "The Battle of Barcelona."

OF GLORY...

Above: The European Cup-Winners' Cup trophy.
Left: Willie Johnston rises between two Russian defenders to head his first and Rangers' second goal.

Quote . . . from Rangers' boss Willie Waddell (now General Manager — shown above) . . .
"Rangers displayed a quality that Bayern Munich, rated favourites for this trophy, lacked. They had courage to go with well-disciplined ability. I must admit to feeling worried when the score went to 3-2 because Dynamo were really going at us then. But the fighters, the wreckers and the hooligans disgraced Rangers and Scotland in Barcelona. They may have been wearing Rangers' colours but underneath they are still hooligans."
Quote . . . from Moscow Dynamo Manager Konstanin Beskov.
"The lives of my players were in danger when Rangers' supporters invaded the pitch. Now we must protest to U.E.F.A. who should order this Final to be replayed."
Quote . . . from two-goal hero Willie Johnston.
"Those fans could have cost us the game and the Cup."

AFTERMATH

FOLLOWING a meeting in June, 1972, U.E.F.A. stated that Rangers could keep the trophy but they would be banned from all competitive European football for two years because of the bad behaviour of a section of their fans.

However, Rangers appealed and the ban was later cut to one year. The ban was estimated to have cost the club well over £100,000.

Above: After the match delirious Rangers fans invaded the pitch. Here Colin Stein runs the human gauntlet.
Right: Skipper John Greig with the Cup which had to be presented to the team in the safety of the dressing-room.

HOTSHOT they call him. The man with the hardest shot in football. The player who is dangerous even 40 yards from goal. That's Leeds and Scotland marksman Peter Lorimer, the forward with dynamite in his boots.

He says: "If I catch the ball right, there isn't a goalkeeper in the world who can hold my shot."

That's more fact than a boast. But Peter is not just a pretty boot! He also knows how to leave defenders stranded . . . as Birmingham's Tommy Carroll found out here.

Yes, Peter is quite a player, with quite a shot. Tommy Carroll was lucky . . . he was better off than the Birmingham goalkeeper!

FRANCIS LEE
(Manchester City)

G-O-A-L!

What a leap! And there's nothing Chelsea's David Webb (above, right) can do about it as Liverpool's Welsh international striker John Toshack soars into orbit and heads home a great goal at Anfield.

ABOVE: Another rocket hurtles goal-wards, this time from West Ham midfield maestro Trevor Brooking (grounded). Pity poor Palace 'keeper Paul Hammond.

LEFT: Manchester City custodian Joe Corrigan can't prevent this header from Leeds' Trevor Cherry (white shirt, centre) finding the net.

OPPOSITE PAGE, BELOW: Try and stop that one! Stoke's Jimmy Greenhoff (stripes, right) cracks in a bullet of a shot against a luckless Birmingham side at the Victoria Ground. No wonder 'keeper David Latchford appears to be gasping in disbelief!

RIGHT: Wolves 'keeper Phil Parkes looks stricken with horror as Manchester City ace Rodney Marsh (right) prods this one in against the Molineux side at Maine Road.

TAKE that! Rangers sharpshooter Alex MacDonald sends a shot flying towards the Celtic goal despite the attention of (from left) Bobby Murdoch, Pat McCluskey, Kenny Dalglish, Tommy Callaghan and Billy McNeill. Alex's team-mate Jim Denny stands by.

Published by IPC Magazines Ltd., Fleetway House, Farringdon Street, London, England.
Sole agents for Australia and New Zealand, Gordon & Gotch Ltd.;
South Africa, Central News Agency Ltd.; Rhodesia and Zambia, Kingstons Ltd.
Printed in England by Fleetway Printers, Gravesend, Kent.

85037-084-1